A History of
ROBIN HOOD'S BAY

The Story of
A Yorkshire Community

BY
BARRIE FARNILL

with photographs from
the Robin Lidster Collection

For Mary and Stephen

First published 1966
Revised and reprinted 1990 and 2004
© North York Moors National Park 1990
© Photographs – J. Robin Lidster
ISBN 1 904622 04 6 (enlarged edition)
(ISBN 0 907480 22 5 1990 edition)

CONTENTS

This book has been produced with funding from the Nortrail Project which is creating a walking trail around the countries of the North Sea – Norway, Sweden, Denmark, Germany and the Netherlands as well as England and Scotland.

Nortrail links walking opportunities with the rich and often common natural and cultural heritage of the North Sea countries. This book provides just one example of this, as it identifies the strong Scandinavian influences on the development of Robin Hood's Bay.

PREFACE

Barrie Farnill was the Assistant Editor (Features) of the Yorkshire Evening Post and a President of the Institute of Journalists. Born in Leeds, he lost count of the number of holidays spent in Robin Hood's Bay many years before beginning to research this book in the early 1960s. A specialist in travel writing, he heard people speak nostalgically of Robin Hood's Bay in places as far distant as Ontario and the Ukraine.

The book was first published in 1966 and was revised for the 1990 edition. It is extensively illustrated with photographs from the collection of J. Robin Lidster who takes a keen interest in the history of Robin Hood's Bay.

In recent years there have been many changes in Robin Hood's Bay so a final chapter, written by Alan Staniforth, has been added. Alan worked for the North York Moors National Park Authority for 30 years, latterly as the Heritage Coast Ranger.

FOREWORD

lthough for many years I have made my home in Cornwall, my roots remain deep in my 'near' native village of Robin Hood's Bay. I say 'near' for I was born in Shipley. I was one year old when first I sniffed the good air of the North Sea. That was a long time ago, long enough you might think to justify my claim to be somewhat of an authority on the place. I am indeed old enough to remember the days when more than thirty fishermen followed their calling in their sturdy, gaily painted cobles the whole year round — line fishing, crab and lobstering, and salmoning — when for every steamboat moving along the off-shore traffic lane, there'd be as many brigs and schooners, some of them Bay owned and manned.

Occasionally, such a vessel, northward bound for the Tees or Tyne from the Continent would drop anchor. Her skipper, with members of her crew at the oars, would pull ashore in the ship's boat, bringing discreetly wrapped parcels to be handed over to relatives waiting on the Landing Scaur. The coastguard on duty in the watch house at Wayfoot would turn a Nelson's eye, but beyond doubt there would be at least one bottle of cognac and other dutiable articles in cottage cupboards that night.

Old customs die hard! Smuggling at the Bay was one of them. In the past Baymen were notorious for their participation in a well organised business, which despite its risks must have paid better than fishing. They must have been exciting times, but how exciting I never realised until I read Barrie Farnill's fascinating book.

Until now there has been no authentic and detailed record of Bay's involvement in smuggling: of the chases, the fights between smugglers and preventive men at sea and on shore; the landing of cargoes, and the night riders over the moors.

The author may not have the advantage of having been (nearly) born and bred in t'awd spot, but his affection for it goes back many years, and this is a book written with love. He has written a concise history of the Bay from earliest geological times to the present day. Like myself, he bemoans many of the changes that have taken place in the course of time, notably the complete decline of fishing, and the erosion of the sea which has caused the destruction of many of its cottages. But intrinsically its beauty and fascination remain. In so many ways this book is a testament of love, a book to treasure.

Leo Walmsley
Fowey, 1966

INTRODUCING THE BAY

obin Hood's Bay lies six miles south of Whitby, and fourteen north of Scarborough. Its red-roofed cottages perch on a cliff and around a stream-cut ravine, tucked well into the northern arm of a bay which, sweeping in a miles-wide curve from Ness Point to the mighty Ravenscar cliffs, is one of the loveliest on England's east coast. Behind it the land rises steeply several hundred feet high to Fylingdales moor. In old Baytown and its environs, which together form the 'capital' of Fylingdales parish, live permanently well over 1,000 people. The village is also full of ghosts, kindly and gentle reminders of a colourful, and at times stormy past. It is also much visited by its adopted sons and daughters, who obey its silent power of recall again and again after their first visit; until one day they begin using, unconsciously, the native's affectionate diminutive − 'Bay' − and that is a sign that they, too, now 'belong Bay'.

The charm of Bay is infectious. It will never leave you and once having conquered, becomes even more subtle. Time spent here has a strangely different pace and quality, so strong are the links with the old long-vanished community of remarkable people.

By any standard, this is an attractive place. The quaint houses appear to be marching down to the shore, leaning on one another's shoulders. It was a common ambition among fisherwives to leave a cosy cottage in the old village for a red brick villa in the sprawling suburb at the top of steep Bay Bank, but fifty years ago perhaps the workaday fishing village did not look as pretty to their eyes. The old fishing cobles have long since disappeared. On occasion there are one or two small boats drawn up in The Dock, and at weekends often a sail upon the water. But those that launch their craft from Wayfoot do so for the simple pleasures of wind and tide on a nearly calm day. Sometimes a local man pushes out a dinghy and later, for those in the know, there is fresh boiled Bay lobster, or in season, delicious sea trout.

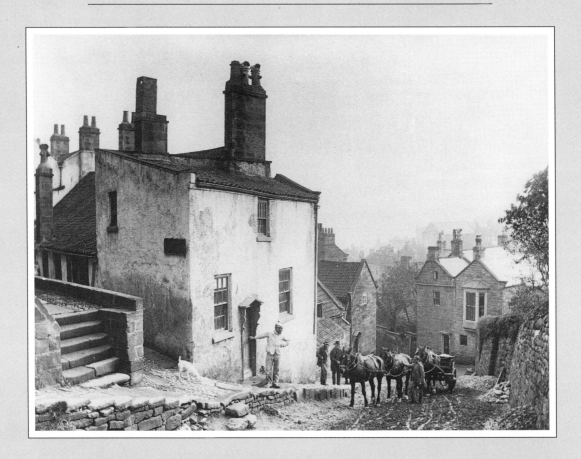

Bay Bank in the 1880s (Sutcliffe)

Bay Bank

The story of Robin Hood's Bay is not ended yet. Much of it is also inextricably woven into the story of Fylingdales. For much of its course, the story is of a running fight betweeen the villagers and the sea. Sometimes they fought intruding strangers, such as the Press Gang, revenue men, and dragoons. But for most of their days they fought the sea. They were a proud, brave, industrious people here, cousins to the oarsmen who sailed to this coast from Scandinavia fourteen centuries ago. Today, when the diesel engine and the glowing eye of the radar scanner serve the north east coast fishermen each night, there are countless interesting reminders of the old communities, and of their courage and skill.

Where should we begin the story of Robin Hood's Bay? If you stroll on the beach you will see some of the early story for yourself, for these cliffs are among the most richly fossiliferous in Britain. Search for ten minutes and you will find an ammonite, or you might, like university students in 1961, find a prehistoric monster, the giant lizard-like *plesiosaurus*. Both are many millions of years old. Man first left a lasting mark here about 3,000 years ago by making huge burial grounds looking down on the present village from the high moorland a mile or so south. These we call Robin Hood's Butts, but Bronze Age man dug them. Some 1,500 years later, Roman soldiers had a stone signal tower at Ravenscar. The first regular settlers were probably Saxon peasants. After them came the Norsemen, some by sea, and others overland. Their descendants, after two score generations, were the fishermen who feared little save an empty line or net. Others were to make a more profitable living out of wading through the surf and onto the moor, with a five gallon cask of smuggled brandy, or a bag of tea on their shoulders. Then came a breed of solemn square-bearded mariners, taking sail to the four corners of the earth. Later generations served in the Merchant Navy.

The 19th century fishermen would have scorned any idea that Bay's was a romantic story, as they busily barrelled cod and ling on a cold day, wearing sealskin caps. They lived at the latter end of the most dramatic period in the community's history, during which for many years the bay was a base for heavily armed smuggling vessels which fought a running sea war with the King's customs cutters. The bulk of the 18th century smuggling took place on the south east coast, but the Yorkshire coast had its share, and the busiest smuggling community on it was that of Robin Hood's Bay. Its natural isolation, protected by marshy moorland on three sides, was a natural aid to the lawless. Something of their doings are recorded in ancient archives,

Barrelling Fish

'… fishermen would have scorned any idea that
Bay's was a romantic story as they busily barrelled
cod and ling on a cold day'.

which together with information from other sources, give a clear picture of the smuggling era. Most of the tales about the old free-traders, with their wealthy sponsors, their highly organised gangs of landsmen, and their connections with Continental entrepots, are lost for ever.

Finally, one of the most oft-repeated tales about Robin Hood's Bay is its supposed connection with the outlaw of Sherwood Forest. Legend says he founded the town. But there is stronger evidence to suggest that in fact those men who were among the first to dwell in the area were directly responsible for suggesting a name to their inheritors, thousands of years later.

LIFE THROUGH THE AGES

The beautiful vista of cliff and sea has taken a thousand ages to mould, and a close search of the rocks can produce dramatic links with the dawn of life. For anyone with the slightest interest in geology, the shore is a treasure trove. It has been called the graveyard of the Jurassic age. About 220 million years ago, when the great warm European swamps were sinking to form coal deposits, they were the homes of strange creatures, some like small crocodiles, others like large newts. There were winged insects up to two feet long, and vegetation included huge trees and great ferns. While the age of giant reptiles was dying, there swam in these warm waters the last of the plesiosaurs, creatures with long tapering tails and long necks with small heads.

One day in 1961, a geology student from Manchester broke off from the cliff near Ravenscar what he first took to be a stick. Later he and his friends began to poke about the rock excitedly. The 'stick' was part of the skull of a fossilised plesiosaur — the whole of which is now in Manchester University — discovered perhaps some 125 million years after the creature expired at the bottom of a prehistoric pool.

The old village rests on mud banks which in turn rest on the Lias. This is quarrymen's dialect for layers because the stratification is plain to see. They consist of alternate beds of limestone and blue shale. The long scaurs exposed at low tide were formed about 170 million years ago in a deep sea which covered what is now the Yorkshire coast. Mud was washed down and pressurised into rock.

The sea animals of the time were buried in it to become the fossils found in many of the rock beds. Many elementary books on geology will explain the rock strata and the fossils to be found here. Whitby Museum has a splendid selection of the latter.

The larger fossilised sea animals are not very common, but there are millions of the smaller ones lying around. Coral fossil, tiny shells, the crayon-shaped belemnite, and, of course, spiral-shaped ammonites are plentiful. The folk of the Middle Ages thought these were the remains of actual serpents miraculously petrified by St. Hilda. Their name comes from the classical god Jupiter Ammon, whose head wore ram's horns, which the shells resemble. The ammonites died out 60 million years ago, but a cousin known as the Pearly Nautilus lives still in the warm waters of the Indian Ocean. It is related to both the octopus and the cuttlefish, and has tentacles to grasp its prey. It builds a beautifully coiled spiral shell, divided by partitions which it extends as it grows larger, and so of course, did the ammonite.

The sandstones nearer Ravenscar were laid down in the dense primeval swamps by muddy streams, and they preserve the remains of ferns and animals. Thin coal seams which can be seen in the cliffs below Ravenscar are the remnants of very dense areas of vegetation.

During the Ice Age the bay became the outlet for a south-moving glacier which dragged boulder clay with it. This forms the soft crumbling cliff to the south of the village. This glacial debris also brought smooth-ground pebbles, coloured grey, green, pink and other shades by different mineral content. Some have come from as far distant as Scotland and Norway. Stretching back inland behind Robin Hood's Bay is an intricate network of valleys, some carved by the over-flowing water of a glacial lake. The Ice Age, which had lasted for hundreds of years, ended about 10,000 years ago, and the giant ice cap, which had stretched down to the Thames, finally melted. Then the sea waves took a hand in sculpting the scene. They pounded the coast with an abrasive mixture of water and sand, rasping steadily at the surface, and gradually cutting back the land by undermining the strata, making the summits collapse, exposing the rocks. Finally came the rain, draining off the land to form a rushing stream which cut the present ravine leading down to the shore. The bay was empty and alone — waiting for man.

There might have been early Stone Age men in this district when there was no sea here at all, but merely a dense coniferous forest extending from the Pennines to the Urals. About 10,000 years ago there was a small settlement at Star Carr, near Scarborough, and flint axes found at Ravenscar are of the type introduced from Denmark about 6,000 years ago. These settlers would be skin-clad people hunting for their food, and moving from camp to camp on heathery islands above the marshy forests, before the general rise in ocean levels finally separated Britain from the Continent about 4,000 BC. In about 2,000 BC the Whitby area was invaded by the Beaker people, known by this name because of their pottery. They were from central Europe, had mingled with nomads from South Russia and sailed from Holland and Germany in dug-out canoes. Some of their descendants may well have built the grave mounds on the high ground almost two miles south from the village and clearly visible against the sky. Many barrows or tumuli are found in this district. The Bronze Age people who left the barrows may have cleared land to keep cattle and sheep. They might have been star worshippers, and there is something moving in their attempts to provide a lasting dignity for their dead.

Canon John Christopher Atkinson, the famous priest-scholar of Danby, near Whitby, wrote in 1891:

> 'Cannot one see the toiling tribesmen, labouring for days and weeks maybe, raising that mighty mound we call Robin Hood's Butt, ninety-five feet in diameter and seventeen or eighteen high, basketful by basketful, almost handful by handful, brought together with infinite pains and care, and strewed symmetrically with accurate adjustment. One cannot but allow for the presence of very potent considerations and very strong and sustained feelings in the breasts of the people who acted thus. Whatever their belief or their superstition (if we are sectarian enough to allow them for nothing better) they were capable of acting in concert, of a great respect for the dead, of a conviction that life was not yet totally at an end, even for their cremated or inhumed fore elders, relatives, friends and leaders. There might be, there probably was, fear as well as respect or reverence mixed up with the funeral rites and observances. There might be, almost certainly there was, an idea of purification in the fire wherein the body was burned.'

Canon Atkinson pointed out that without a potter's wheel the cremators made sepulchral vases up to twenty-five inches high and eighteen inches in diameter, graceful and firm enough to withstand the rigours of thousands of years in the soil. The barrow of which he spoke, when excavated many years ago, disclosed a cinerary urn which can now be seen in the Rotunda Museum, Scarborough. It is about fourteen inches high and nine or ten inches in diameter, having a large lip and a herring bone pattern on the upper portion. Within the urn were found flint knives and fragments, and a bone pin. The approximate date of the urn is thought to be 1,400 to 800 BC.

Bronze Age Urn

Middle Bronze Age Collared Urn decorated with
geometric patterns impressed by twisted cord, from
Robin Hood's Butts, South Barrow, Fylingdales Moor
(Rotunda Museum, Scarborough)

Whether the Urn people survived the invasion from Gaul in the 3rd century BC by the ancestors of the Brigantes is not known. Some authorities think the moors were emptied by that time as the climate was growing colder. The Romans probably brought the first civilisation to the bay. Though Caesar landed in Kent in AD 58, it was probably not until the end of the 4th century AD that a Roman military post was established at Ravenscar. In 1771, builders' men excavating on the site of what is now Raven Hall Hotel, found a stone which is now in Whitby Museum. The inscription has been translated: 'Justinian, governor of the province, and Vindicianus, prefect of soldiers, built this fort'.

Probably the Romans built the same type of three-storey signal tower as there was at Scarborough, part of a chain extending from Filey to Goldsborough, several miles north of Whitby, and perhaps to County Durham. These small forts were to watch the sea-lanes for Saxon pirates and to pass messages down the coast to the Humber, the possible anchorage of a Roman fleet. From Ravenscar's 600 feet high cliffs, can be seen thirty miles out to sea on a clear day. The Yorkshire signal towers were thought to be occupied until about AD 395, being then destroyed by fresh invaders.

After the Anglo Saxon invaders came the Danes and the land-starved Norwegians. The Saxons preferred to settle by rivers and Whitby may have attracted them more, but some Anglian pottery was found in Fylingdales and is now in the Yorkshire Museum. The origin of the name Fylingdales is believed to be the old English word *fygela,* which referred to marshy ground. The *Figelinge* of Domesday probably included the series of small valleys which met the sea in Robin Hood's Bay.

This kind of word history can be fascinating. Stoupe Brow, a hill to the south of Robin Hood's Bay, has an informative derivation. Stoupe is from the old Norse word *staup* meaning steep; the suffix is old English or West Saxon *bru* meaning brow. Stoupe was spelled as Staupe as late as 1133. Other names from the West Saxon language in this are include Raw, a row (of houses), and Ness, meaning a headland. The familiar word scaur, given to ribs of rock stretched seawards, comes from old Norse *sker* meaning rock. A Wyke was a *vik* or sea-creek. The rushing becks take their name from *bec* — a stream. Dale is from *dalr* meaning valley. Toft means dwelling, while holm was a water meadow or low lying land. Foss means a force of water or waterfall. Through the years *fjall* became fell, and *tjarn,* tarn. Everywhere you turn in this part of North Yorkshire the language of the Viking has outlasted him by

Robin Hood's Bay

Aquatint by F. Nicholson, 1828

a thousand years and more. This would have pleased the old sea warriors who had firm faith in their own immortality!

Other Scandinavian names near Fylingdales include Ugglebarnby, which was *uglubardi* (Owl Beard's Farm). *Haugr* was the name for a burial mound, and became howe. Thus Jugger (*Jaeger*) Howe, on Fylingdales Moor, is the grave of the hunter. Thorpe was Danish for an outlying holding apart from the main estate. Fyling Thorpe, or Preste Thorpe as it was once known, the village adjacent to Robin Hood's Bay, belonged to the monks of Whitby. *By* was the word for a small settlement or farm.

From what is Ravenscar derived? The Raven was the emblem of the Norsemen, the god Odin's secret bird which flew off his shoulder to warn him of what went on in the world. Ravenscar is the revival of an old name (the district was known as Peak for a long time) and may well mean 'rock of the raven' or where the Vikings planted their flag. On the other hand, it has been suggested that the name is Celtic, and refers to the sea-coast situation.

The north east of Yorkshire was thickly populated by the Norwegian colonists. Oswald Harland, writing in *Yorkshire, North Riding*, puts it succinctly:

> 'All down the coast from Saltburn to Filey and beyond, the village folk live in fierce detached shyness. Their Viking blood is still strong-running. They are a silent dour people, busy among shorewrack and seajunk, nets, crab-pots, boats, tackle and such.'

Norwegian and Dane found the terrain much like their own at home. They built wooden and turf homes and settled down. The Danes did not settle in the Whitby area much. The Norwegians were the main colonists. The thought of Norse longships flying into the bay at ten knots with up to one hundred men underneath each broad sail of blue, red or green, looking eagerly for their new homeland, would be a romantic one, but perhaps not wholly accurate. Although some Norwegians did enter direct from the sea, many of them walked across England from the north west, having been evicted from Ireland. They occupied big tracts of South West Scotland and North West England, and by the 10th century there was an abundance of Norwegian place names in Cumberland, Westmorland, Lancashire, Northumberland and Yorkshire. Why did they come to what was later Robin Hood's Bay? Fertile soil was the lodestone: the rich brown glacial soil of Fylingdales.

The Viking invasions of Europe lasted for two centuries, and though some were little more than pirate raids, there were many colonisers among the armies, for the invaders were skilled farmers and metal workers as well as fighters. They left a lasting mark on the North Riding, which is itself a survival of the original Scandinavian *thrithing* or a third. Johannes Bronsted, the Norwegian historian, describes his Viking ancestors as: 'Polygamous, daring, adventurous, scornful of death, a powerful and dangerous race'. However, he opined that there was little reason to believe that the Anglo Saxons were pushed out or enslaved by the Viking colonists, though the invaders probably helped themselves to substantial properties. This subsequent racial mixture then, was the far-back ancestry of many north east coast fisherfolk.

Just as in the 9th century, the prayer rose from France's northern convents: 'Save us, O God, from the violence of the men from the North', so the same cry was probably echoed on the coast of North Yorkshire. For the Viking raids of 867 destroyed the wooden-walled monastery of the great Abbess-Princess Saint Hilda at Whitby, 200 years after its foundation, and it was another 200 years before it was rebuilt.

Very likely the Norsemen who made their home in Fylingdales did so in the forests around what is now the hamlet of Raw, to avoid detection by other pirates. There is no record of their doings here. A Viking axe has been found a mile or so away at Hawsker — a Nordic enough name in itself — but local archaeological evidence of the Vikings is slender. We may surmise that while the Viking armies were still battling round Europe, there existed here a small Viking settlement, its members tilling the land as well as sailing small fishing craft modelled on the old longship. It may well have been the beginnings of the 11th century before lasting peace descended on the colonists. Whenever it was, the lives of these farmer-fishermen in their rough huts set the pattern for many centuries to come.

In 1016 Eric of Norway sat as earl over the Northumbrian provinces, and in 1041, Siward, a Danish warrior earl, ruled. On the latter's death in 1055 he was succeeded by Tostig, brother of King Harold. Tostig, who was also kinsman to William of Normandy, was banished overseas by Harold as a dangerous rival, but he returned to Yorkshire dramatically. Taking refuge in Norway, he secured the aid of the Viking warrior King Harold Hardrada, and these two fell upon the Yorkshire coast with an army and were killed at Stamford Bridge on September 25th, 1066, after laying waste the coastline between Cleveland and Spurn.

Before William of Normandy conquered England, the manor of Fyling was held by one Merewin, with one carucate of land (about 160 acres). After the Conquest the land was part of the spoils of the war given to one of William's relatives, Hugh of Chester. Later, the revolt against William in 1068 may or may not have been the end of the small settlement. In revenge for the slaughter of 3,000 Normans at the York garrison, William burned towns and villages, especially on the coast, and famine followed the destruction of crops, cattle, and even farm tools. Fyling, surrounded by marshy forest, might have escaped the 'Harrying of the North'.

The Domesday survey of 1086 refers to 'waste' after the names of many Yorkshire towns and villages. It does so referring to the Manor of Whitby and Sneaton, which included Fylingdales. The Manor then belonged to Earl Hugh of Chester, possibly a nephew of the Conqueror, and was ruled by William Perci, one of the invading nobles. It included 'Figelinge, one carucate, Nortfigeling (probably Fylingthorpe) five carucates'. Fyling, often referred to as South Fyling, might well be the site later occupied by either Fyling Park or Fyling Hall. North Fyling, with its five carucates, was the largest of eleven places mentioned in the Manor. *The Domesday Book* continues:

> 'In all 28 carucates of six borates for geld and 24 ploughs may be (there). Earl Hugh has these and William (de Perci) of him. Nearly all waste. Only in Prestebi (on Whitby Abbey site) and Sourebi there are two ploughs in the demesne and eight sokemen with one plough and 30 villanes with three ploughs and one mill of 10s annual value and 26 acres of meadow.'

(A carucate, a Danelaw measurement, varied between 160 and 180 acres, or as much as an eight-ox team could plough in a year. A borate, or bovate, was one eighth of a carucate). From this, it seems that North Fyling, with its five carucates could have had as much as 900 acres of cleared land.

The geographical development of the early communities in the dale are suggested by the position of St. Ive's chapel site, the first known place of worship. This is well over a mile inland and is 500 feet above sea level, almost equidistant from Fyling Hall and Thorpe. Its position would indicate it served a once widespread community rather than a coastal settlement. The later site of the 12th century church at Raw, over a mile away from St. Ives, suggests the population centre shifted, perhaps with the growth of fishing, to nearer the sheltered water offered by the headland, Ness Point. Eventually the reborn religious house at Whitby began to exert a strong influence here. One of the Conqueror's officers, Reinfrid, was so appalled at the ruin he had helped to create in the wasting of the North that he became a monk and helped found another Whitby Abbey 200 years after the Vikings destroyed it. He became the first Prior of Whitby Abbey, which was founded by William de Percy. Canon Atkinson mentions that William de Percy was tenant in the *capite* of Whitby and its *maneria* and *sokes*, but before he could round off his endowment of the new Abbey he had to buy back Fylingdales from Tancred the Fleming, who evidently had the estate by grant or concession of either the Earl or William himself.

After this financial arrangement, followed by Tancred's return to his native land, William granted to the monastery the:

> '*vill and seaport of Whitby, numerous places including Fieling and the other Fieling, the Church of St. Mary of Whitby together with its chapels, Fyling, Hawsker, Sneaton, Ugglebarmy, Dunaby and Aislaby, several mills including Fyling Mill.*'

The vaccaries (cattle farms) of Stoup, and Thornely (probably Thorny Brow) are also mentioned. Altogether the Abbot of Whitby held twenty to thirty thousand acres of the land.

William de Percy was evidently a most religious man. He founded the Abbey, and in 1096 went on the Crusades and died on the march in Jerusalem in that year. His nephew, William de Percy, became the first Abbot. Alan de Percy, his son, ratified and confirmed by charter his father's gift of Fyling lands (both North and South) together with Normandby and *Hauckesgard* (Hawsker). Forced under the powerful influence of a new and great religious house by the piety of a French baron, who himself probably had Viking blood from Normandy, the ordinary folk of the dale did what ordinary folk do anywhere when there is a change at the top. They got on with the job: they fished and farmed. Daily life probably altered little through the succeeding two or three centuries.

'A fischer tounelet of 20 bootes with Dok or Bosom of a mile yn length.' This is the first description of Robin Hood's Bay, applied by King Henry VIII's topographer Leland in 1536. Gradually the cliff village had grown larger, perhaps because men found it less convenient to walk daily to their boats from the inland settlements. Very likely the present village originated in the 15th century, because by 1540 it is said there were fifty cottages by the shore. The first homes there would have been hovels by the standard of even

Robin Hood's Bay from the North

the later small, cramped, and damp houses. The medieval villager built with timber and wattle and daub — a framework of interlaced twigs daubed with clay and lime and horsehair or cowhair. Through a hole in the straw thatch, smoke would wind from the open hearth. Probably very few buildings were built in both timber and stone until the 16th century.

Robin Hood's Bay was a far more important place than Whitby in the 16th century, according to an early mariners' chart. In Rotterdam's Prince Hendrik's Maritime Museum is the Mariner's Mirror, a series of old North Sea charts published in 1586 by Waghenaer, describing the coasts of Europe. *Robinhoodes Bay* is indicated, together with a compass course from Rotterdam, some 275 miles away. Whitby is not mentioned, although about thirty other European ports are listed. The village is marked with a tiny picture of tall houses with gabled roofs and by it is the drawing of an anchor.

If there is an explanation of the development of the bay as a fishing centre and an anchorage for shipping it cannot be that it offered a better haven than the River Esk, four miles to the north, with its broad beaches at either side, and sheltered anchorage. The latter's navigational advantages should have scored over the rocky shore of Robin Hood's Bay, where there is only a narrow channel between two scaurs over which to creep up to the cliff bottom. Perhaps there was heavy silting at Whitby, with little channel and an enforced open anchorage. Perhaps the fishing prospects were better off the bay.

There are only fragments of historical records with which to bridge long periods of time in the Fylingdales story. Life cannot have altered radically between the 11th and 16th centuries. The Abbey landlords would exert a powerful influence. The economic and social system spreading from the Abbey, with its careful delineations of power and property, and its attention to the Royal laws, would be like a stabilising anchor on the lives of many succeeding generations.

The Abbey's tenants paid their rent mostly by rendering service to the monks. In the early part of the 12th century, the bondsmen of Stoup Silpho and South Fyling held one borate of land each, paying one shilling rent. All had to grind their corn at the monk's mill in Fyling, paying as multure (commission) one-thirteenth of the quantity ground. Each had to give two fowls and a score of eggs to the monks at Easter, except the Stoup bondsmen, who had to give four fowls and a score and a half of eggs. Perhaps they had better land than the rest.

In almost every case tenants were bound to give four days ploughing, four days harrowing, four hoeing or weeding to the Abbey, and to find eight men to do a day's reaping if they held over twenty acres (Canon Atkinson thought the farms would be from twelve acres up to thirty five acres). Aid had to be given towards stacking corn or hay, or leading loads of wood and turf for the monks. There was a *gildehus* at Fylingdales at this time. It was composed of small farmers, an early form of trade guild.

In the early years there must have been continual readjustments in land tenure. A second surrender of South Fyling to the Abbey took place in 1148 when the land was rendered by Robert, son of William de Aketon and William his son. Aketon might be an old spelling of Egton, near Whitby. There is however, an Aketon near Harrogate, where members of the Percy family, one of whom founded the Abbey, had a seat. Later it is recorded that William, son of Robert of Sicklinghall, gave to Abbot Roger (1222—1224) one mark of rent which he used to receive from the monks for property in South Fyling. (Sicklinghall is only a few miles from Aketon, but there may be no connection). In 1277 Abbot Gilbert claimed one messuage (land including a building or dwelling house) and about forty acres of land in North Fyling.

An early 14th century tax register of the Libertas de Whiteby suggests the group of Fylingdale farms was the largest for miles around. In 1327 William de Sheffelde, making a tax return of those men worth ten shillings, recorded that in *Fighling* were Henrico Parkour, Rogero de Turmyr and seven others, a total of nine. At Stoup cum Thirnhagh (Stoupe Browe and Thornhowe) were Willelmo, son of Ricardo, Willelmo Todde, Simon Hird, Waltero son of Beatrice and three others, a total of seven. This makes a total of sixteen in the two communities living side by side, compared with seven such tenants at Riswarpe (Ruswarp), the same number at Sneaton, and eight at both Ugilbardy (Ugglebarnby) and at Sleights. In 1395 the monks had a mill and a lime kiln at Fylingdales. At this time the Abbot had his deer park here. It was mentioned in 1404 and there are some of the ancient walls still standing at Park Hill, near Thorpe. In 1395 the monks recorded spending twelve pence for a pot at their Fyling limekiln. Other expenses were seventeen pence for a fishing net, and sixpence to feed six reapers. Two shillings were paid to Richard Cras for 'three little pigs before the Nativity' and the same man sold the monks seven hens at twopence each.

Such small amounts as six old pence (2½p) for feeding six men, and a hen for twopence (less than 1p) underline the ravages of latterday inflation, though some claim this process has existed since Ancient Greece.

Brother William de Dalton, the Bursar, in the year 1396-7 made the following ledger entries:

Fylingdales

For the farm of Sothfyling	*40s*
For the court there (profits from the manor court)	*6s*
Services of vassals (money paid by them in lieu of work)	*3s*
Services of ploughing	*2s 6d*
Cow land at Maiderscow	*8s 6d*
Helwath	*7s 6d*
Profits of the Mill	*20s*

Other receipts during that year included the sum of £5 17s for the farm of Northfyling, £1 11s 8d for the one at Stowpe, and £1 4s for Thyrnaw farm.

A survey of the monastic lands in 1536 mentions the monks owning, among other properties, Fyling manor, and farms, at an annual value of £25 9s 9d, Fyling Grange (now Old Fyling Hall) *Fylinge Milne,* and other properties including *Mige Hall* and a messuage called *Middilwood Halle.* There is a Middlewood farm at the bay today, and a small house called Midge Hall at Falling Foss, much further inland. The monks also owned *Robinhoode Bay,* and its *herynge house* (The herring house was kept by John Smith from Wakefield). They had property over a wide area, as far away in fact as Scarborough.

In Henry VIII's reign it was deemed:

> '*very necessary that all the woods within the parish of Whitby or elsewhere therunto, shall be reserved for the maintenance of the King's cottages in Whitby and at Robyn Hood's Baye.*'

Later Queen Elizabeth disposed of fifty of her tenements at the bay. The stream running through the village is still called King's Beck, and of course, there is King Street.

In 1540, the year after the Abbey was surrendered by the last abbot, Henry Daval, the chief tenant at Robin Hood's Bay was Matthew Storme, who rented Cow Close at £1 18s 4d per year. Among the names there were John, Peter, William, Robert and Bartholomew Storm. (Four centuries later there were still sixteen Storms living in the village). Other tenants were John and Christopher Maltby, John Iddle, George Grindale, John Cockerell, Thomas Marsigale, Robert Doocheman, Agnes Salmon, and Agnes, wife of Robert Morssone. Fyling Raw was occupied by John and

Thomas Huntrodes. Also in Fylingdales in 1540 were two men named Allatson who, perhaps, gave their name to Allison's wood, lying south of the village.

A unique legacy of the Abbey is the penny hedge ceremony, carried out at Whitby the day before Ascension Day. For very many years it was carried out by members of the Hutton family of Fylingdales, and at one time recently lapsed for a year or two, but has now been re-commenced. The ceremony consists of driving a number of stakes into the shore at low tide, so fixed that they stand for three tides. It is thought to be the continuation of a ceremony in which the Abbot's boundaries were marked annually by tradition. The Penny Hedge is also known as the Horngarth. Garth is old Danish for fence, and the horn probably alludes to horned stock, or cows and oxen.

The Abbot's book records:

> 'Everie yeer the Horngarth service ys to be doone upon Hollie thursday even. Tho. Cockrill being Bayliff to the Abbot, did meete by sonn-rise the Conieres, the Strangewayes, the Eldringtenes, and Alletsons, who were bound to this service. In the Strye-head End by Lytellbeck, and the said Cockerill did see everie one cutt downe with a knife, (he appointing the wood) so much as he would serve. From thence they came not the nearest way, but bringing theym upon theyr back went a good way before they came into the way. So comminge to the water at the towne end, they maid the hedge which should stand three tides and then the officer did blow oute upon theyem.'

A traditional legend says that in 1159 three members of local families, Percy, Bruce and Allatson, killed a priest in his cell because he sheltered a wild boar they were hunting in the forest near Whitby. The penalty for killing a priest was death, but while dying, the monk begged mercy for them under pain of their annual penance which was to be the planting of the hedge at Whitby.

Now the adventurous Elizabethan era was at hand; but the medieval fishermen of Robin Hood's Bay would know little of the times they lived in. Their life would be a rough one; home comforts in the timber and thatched cottages would be limited to a fire and a straw palliasse, with a rush light to see them to bed. The summer evenings they might spend on the beach mending their nets — the winter ones in the ale house. Their talk would be gutteral, more like Danish than modern English, and they would be unused to strangers in their isolation.

DID ROBIN HOOD STAY HERE?

he origin of the name Robin Hood's Bay is a mystery. But of all factors which have contributed towards the village's popularity as a holiday centre, not the least important is its romantic name. As a boy, holidaying nearby, I remember distinctly a feeling of excitement at the mere sight of a white sign board at Hawsker cross-roads pointing towards the sea, bearing that magic name. Could the village, fascinating though it is, have commanded the interest of multitudes had it possessed an uninspiring name like Fishcombe? There is not a scrap of evidence to suggest that Robin Hood visited the bay. His connection with this part of Yorkshire is absent from the ballads, though there is one story of him fishing from Scarborough. We may only surmise, but it would be a mistake to assume such surmise to be completely unprofitable.

Let us look more closely at what facts there are. Firstly, the village does not appear under its present name until the early 16th century, and Robin Hood, assuming at least his existence, lived probably in the late 13th century. So this gap hardly supports the old legend that he used the bay as a retreat. However, it must be remembered that there are other, if lesser known stories about him in the district, one for example about him helping the Abbot of Whitby to repel sea pirates.

It is my belief that the village's name grew naturally enough from folk legends with a local origin, later amplified by the Robin Hood legend which itself originated far away. These folk stories were probably fed and strengthened from time to time through the centuries by local superstition, and Robin Hood's identification with the village may be more complex than at first supposed. But if we wish to assess theories it will pay us to examine more closely not only the legends, but local history. Then, I submit, a linking pattern becomes clearly visible.

The name of Robin Hood's Bay is probably the result of superstition attached to the burial mounds on the moor behind Stoupe Brow before the middle of the 15th century or even earlier. It is also possible that it originated from a true story of 12th century sea raiders at Whitby. It is not impossible that the fishermen who lived here related the old ballads round the fireside like the Norsemen told and re-told their sagas, and called themselves 'Robin Hood's men'. The medieval ballad maker's stories of Robin Hood, passed from person to person, elaborated and magnified, would be fed from perhaps a thousand unconnected sources.

It is likely that the two legends of Robin Hood may both spring from actual events and attempts to explain old beliefs. Canon Atkinson, who studied local history deeply, wrote:

> 'I believe the name is due to folk etymology. Robin Hood was also the name of an ancient forest spirit or elf akin to Robin Goodfellow. It was the name most probably given to the barrows (Robin Hood's Butts on Peak Moors) because he was believed to haunt them. Long after this belief became extinct, people attempted to explain the name by associating it with that of the outlaw and his feats of archery especially as the barrows resemble the mounds of butts behind archery targets.'

This puts the whole matter in a nut-shell.

Unconnected sources feed legends, as Valentine Harris points out in his book *The Truth about Robin Hood* (which, incidentally sheds no light on our particular problem). Mr Harris says:

> 'This is how a folk hero grows, and perhaps the prowess shown here (Robin Hood's) could be applied to the majority of heroes'.

The naming of natural features after a folk hero demonstrated his mythical character, explains Mr Harris. There is a Robin Hood's well several miles away on Fylingdales Moor, a Robin Hood's Close near Whitby, and many instances in other parts of the North of natural features named after the hero of Nottingham Forest.

Canon Atkinson's theory about the name resulting from superstition about the Bronze Age graves is supported by the fact that of all communities, of the Middle Ages — and doubtless much later than this period — the fisherfolk were probably among the most superstitious. But in addition there is the significant suggestion that the slopes south of the village were believed to be haunted. It is implicit in the name of the cave by Mill Beck, which is called Boggle Hole. Boggle, or Boggle Boggart, is an old North Yorkshire expression for a goblin, phantom, or ghost.

There is a traditional story that Richard, Abbot of Whitby, sent for Robin when the outlaw was at Robin Hood's Bay and asked for his help against pirates, promising him a Royal pardon as a reward. One hundred Danish pirates are said to have climbed the cliff carrying the raven's standard. Robin's men rolled boulders on to them, and then used their bows and arrows, killing about seventy pirates and losing nine of their own number. Afterwards the Abbot feasted Robin and his band. Then Robin and Little John mounted the Abbey's tower with the Abbot and shot arrows into the fields a mile or so away. (Robin Hood's stone, near Whitby, is supposed to be where his arrow landed).

This story is related in *The Whitby Magazine* for 1827 as being 'illustrative of some interesting traditional anecdotes current in the district'. Interesting certainly, and traditional without doubt, perhaps current for a very long time – but where could it have originated? It is true that there are fields not far from the Abbey called Robin Hood's Close and Little John's Close, too far away to be seriously considered as a bow shot's distance. These surely fall into the general category of features named after a hero of myth and legend.

What is also intriguingly true is that during the time of the first Abbot Richard (1148 to 1178) the King of Norway did enter Whitby with many ships and robbed the monastery. The old story of Robin Hood and the sea pirates could possibly be founded on this incident.

The traditional legend most quoted is the one that the Whitby historian Charlton related in 1779 as follows:

'In the days of the Abbot Richard, and later his successor (i.e. the end of the 12th century) lived that famous and renowned outlaw Robin Hood, who took from the rich that he might have wherewithall to give to the poor. He many years kept under him a considerable number of men who lived by rapine or plunder. He resided generally in Nottinghamshire or the southern part of Yorkshire. But when his robberies came so numerous and the outcries against him so loud as to alarm the whole nation, parties of soldiers were sent down from London to arrest him. And it was that caring for his safety, he found it necessary to desert his usual haunts, and retreating northward to cross the moors that surround Whitby, where gaining the sea coast he always had in readiness near at hand some small fishing vessels to which he could have refuge if he found himself pursued; for in these, putting out to sea, he looked upon himself as quite secure, and held the *power of England at defiance. The chief place of his resort at these times, to which he communicated his name, and which is still called Robin Hood's Bay, where his boats were generally laid up, is about six miles from Whitby. There he frequently went fishing in the summer season, even when the enemy approached to annoy him. Near here he used butts for long bow practice. In 1771 these were excavated and they had been burying places for the dead, used by our pagan ancestors.'*

It is a pleasant story, and it can be dangerous to dismiss a folk tale out of hand without some proof of its falsity. As an example of this, Mr Harris quotes the taking down of a church pillar in Orkney in 1950 when Magnus, the uncle of Ragnold, was found (so it is believed) with an axe stroke through the skull; precisely the same way in which the ancient Orkney saga said he died a thousand years previously! Is there any foundation possible for the traditional legend quoted by Charlton? An incident involving the brave bowmen of Robin Hood's Bay may have helped the old tale along a bit. The story is told by Robert Take Gaskin in his book *The Old Sea Port of Whitby* (1906).

Gaskin says:

'In 1544 when Scotland was our enemy, Sir Richard Cholmley wrote to the Earl of Shrewsbury, stating that two Scottish ships chased two English small ships in the North Sea and one was pursued to a little town called Robynhodbay. Cholmley wrote: "I did repair thither with all speed thinking to have rescued the said ship from their enemy. Howbeit, before my coming the men of Robynhodbay had set forth three of their boats with a dozen archers in them for the aiding of the said ships. The archers did shoot so well that they did constrain the Scottish boats to go to their ships and fetch more ordinance (long pistols) then the Scotch ship drove the archers back to land."'

The Scotsmen won the English ship, and took eleven lasts of salmon, said Cholmley, who added: 'They have hurt many of the Scotsmen with their arrows and some very sore as they think.' The incident could not have been the origin of the village's name, because of its date, but might it not have played its part in originating the legend quoted by Charlton? Whatever the truth of the matter, no one can prove that Robin Hood did not found the village. That pleases the young, and many of the not so young.

A Time For Smugglers

Two excise cutters, *Mermaid* and *Eagle*, flying blue pennants which showed they were on the King's business, sailed southwards from Whitby one October day in 1774. The breeze was only fair, but large sails, ballooning on long-running bowsprits, carried them at a spanking pace. These craft were built for speed, like those of the smugglers. Hulls, which had little freeboard, were black. Their boats were painted white. Bulwarks were also white, a contrasting black being provided by iron guns.

The cutters rounded Ness point. Waiting for them and swinging into position on their anchor lines off-shore at Robin Hood's Bay, were three other vessels: a big schooner, and two smaller open boats known as shallops. The biggest shallop had a King's cutter's blue pennant hoisted, as was often the impudent custom among smugglers. Fishermen on the shore dropped their nets and watched excitedly.

The gap between the cutters and the moored vessels narrowed. Some of the smugglers were already in position on the rigging. Sails billowed, and on the deck other men hastily worked sweeps to move their craft into position.

The boom of a gunpowder charge echoed around the Bay. One of the schooner's guns was fired, followed by a second. A ball whistled into the sea a yard or two from the leading cutter's bow, and the other tore a large rent through its main-sail. Guns of loud and small voices, including the dry crackling vibrato of musket fire, spoke as one, sending a hail of shot across the blue water. The commander of the leading Excise cutter swung his vessel away, its black stern presenting a smaller target. His companion followed suit. These captains knew when they were out-gunned at Robin Hood's Bay. They were old adversaries, these five commanders. The master of one of the shallops, one of the most notorious smugglers on the coast, had recently surprised *Mermaid* at anchor off Dunstanburgh Castle, on the Northumberland coast, and had made her up anchor and leave. Soon the three smugglers were chasing the cutters back up to the Tees, where because of adverse winds they were forced to lie for over a week.

Dramatic incidents like this, reconstructed from old customs records, were commonplace off the Yorkshire coast for well over a century. Gun battles were frequent in the turbulent history of local smuggling. On a national scale, the free-traders, as the smugglers liked to call themselves, conducted what was virtually a sea war against the Crown, with armed fleets, maintained at enormous cost. While many of the smuggling fraternity operated on the southern and western coasts, the Yorkshire coast had its share, with smuggling centred on Robin Hood's Bay. The smugglers left few personal records; despite their fine seamanship, the vast majority would be illiterate, and their calling tended to make them more secretive than most men. They bequeathed us a mixture of legend and anecdote, and a few terse reports in old customs archives.

The Robin Hood's Bay smugglers consisted of all kinds of men, but broadly speaking, they fell into three categories. Firstly, there were the professional seamen, the carriers who linked the village with the great Continental ports where smugglers from all over the British Isles filled their holds. These were not necessarily Bay men, but equally likely to be from Sussex and Kent. Though smuggling craft and crews came from far-off coasts, it was common for them to carry a local man as 'spot man' to guide them to the exact landing place. Then there were the land smugglers, who distributed the contraband, including the many helpers who spied and watched for the smuggling craft, and carried heavy kegs through the surf all night long for a guinea. Lastly there were the syndicates, who financed the operations with no physical risk to themselves. They chartered the vessels, advanced money for goods, and made handsome profits. Many a North Riding yeoman family has advanced in the world through its secret association with the free-traders.

The Robin Hood's Bay smugglers were typical of their 18th century times, centred on an isolated seafaring community. Its insularity was a big natural advantage to the often hazardous trade. The adventurous epoch of smuggling covered a little more than a century and a half, from about the year 1700.

In the middle of the 18th century, for example, tea, being heavily taxed, cost as much as 35s a pound, though cheaper varieties cost as little as 12s. Tea was highly popular, the poor drinking it as often as the rich. It was preferred to coffee or cocoa. Tea could be bought in Holland for 7d a pound: smuggled

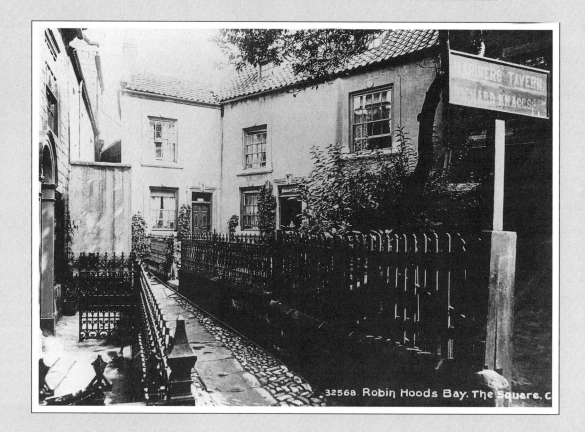

The Mariners Tavern

'... a legendary haunt of the smugglers'.

into England, it could undercut the usual retail price by two-thirds and still make a giant profit. At this time spirits were in keen demand. The well-to-do drank rum and brandy, and the London gin shops, which sold harmful adulterated liquor, were being closed by the Government, leaving ordinary people with a strong taste for gin. Few people, however respectable, had much objection to using contraband goods, provided they escaped detection. Smugglers were often admired, despite the crimes they committed. Tobacco, tea and gin were bought cheerfully by many who would have fiercely resented any imputation of dishonesty.

In 1746 a witness before a Parliamentary commission estimated that out of four million pounds weight of tea consumed in England each year, over three million pounds was smuggled. The drain on the country's finances was enormous. About £1 million annually was taken out of the country to pay for smuggled goods — eighty per cent of which was tea. From Dunkirk and Flushing goods poured into Yorkshire. There was actually a resident colony of Englishmen in Holland trading under 'firm's' names. They were boatbuilders, cask makers and merchants of all kinds. One former English sailor living in Zealand owned four ships and, it was said, smuggled to England half a million pounds of tea annually. Merchants often worked on the basis of one hundred per cent profit. Great distilleries in Holland and France were set up to meet the smugglers' demands and one alone distilled nearly four million gallons of spirit a year, seventy five per cent of it for England. Both France and Holland imported tremendous quantities of tea a year — not for their own population to drink, but for illegal export to England. Even the Napoleonic wars made little difference to the busy trading. Napoleon himself said:

> 'They (the smugglers) have courage and ability to do anything for money. They took from France annually forty or fifty millions worth of silks and brandy.'

Smuggled tobacco, at sixpence a pound, avoided five shillings duty. Dutch tea at sevenpence a pound was sold in England for five shillings; French brandy at five shillings a gallon fetched four times the price in England. No wonder the trade was brisk.

The riding officers of the customs had to be avoided on this side of the sea. Troops were also deployed. The ocean was wide, and the risks of a capture at sea were not high. Men sailed fast craft, usually crossing by night, and revenue cutters were few. In 1784 there was only one at Hull and two at

Newcastle. Faced with a growing problem, the Government took stronger measures and the risks increased. Smuggling vessels in their turn grew larger and more heavily armed, and the land smugglers also grew more violent. Writing in the halcyon days of free trade in 1752 Horace Walpole remarked:

> 'It is shocking to think what a shambles this country is grown. Seventeen were executed this morning.'

Smugglers were not always hanged as they were in mid 18th century. Penalties varied throughout the centuries as Governments struggled with the problem. It was common for them to be deported, or pressed into army or navy services for five years, or jailed. Many of those pressed into men-of-war got quick promotion because they were remarkable sailors, much to the annoyance of the rest. But if the penalties were high, then so were the rewards. In 1738, one skipper admitted to making £250 on one run from Dunkirk to the Yorkshire coast with 2,000 gallons of brandy. Seamen got as much as £5 a run, and labourers a guinea for portering ankers (ten-gallon tubs) on to the beach. The syndicates made a fortune, of course.

Anti-smuggling laws were tightened to the extent that any vessel of over fifty tons rigged as a lugger was liable to forfeiture. As late as 1808 the 'boatmasters and fishermen' of Robin Hood's Bay protested against this law, pointing out that their craft engaged in the Yarmouth herring industry would be affected by it. However, the Customs Board indicated the clause in the Act which allowed their vessels 'which were rigged and fitted at the time of passing thereof and intended for the purpose of fishing' to be licensed. Seized smuggling craft were broken up, and penalties on landsmen were severe. Six months in jail was commonly received by landsmen on mere suspicion of signalling to a smuggling vessel. Finally, a combination of stern legislation, stronger preventive measures, including the fast steam cutter and a big reduction in spirit duties put the freetraders out of business. The profits no longer bore relation to the risks.

The smugglers' vessels traded with many other Yorkshire coastal villages besides Robin Hood's Bay, but the bay was a favourite anchorage for them, a base from which they could outmatch any government force when they gathered in strength. Whenever government vessels approached, the smugglers simply drove them away by superior force. With half the district in league with them, and the other half terrorised into silence, they must have felt, with good reason, that the fishing township was an impregnable fortress. It was impossible to impose any form of law there; and at the peak of the smuggling, the local customs officers were almost certainly bribed to ignore it.

If the keepers of the law were not happy on land, they fared no better at sea. One Newcastle customs cruiser captain recorded that he rarely left port without being fired on. In April, 1777, the Revenue cutter *Swallow*, from Hull, commanded by Captain Mitchell, sighted a famous smuggler in the North Sea. The latter was the 200 ton schooner *Kent*, Dungeness built, and skippered by a man known as 'Stoney'. Captain Mitchell reported in his log:

> *'As their guns were in readiness and at the same time waving us to go to the northward, we were by reason of their superior force obliged to sheer off, but did our best endeavours to spoil his market, there being a large fleet of colliers with him.'*

It was a regular practice for the coal-brigs to rendezvous at sea with the smugglers and take on an additional and illicit cargo. If the winds were right, coastal trading vessels could often make a fast run to the continent for contraband to hide among their cargo.

In the early 18th century, before the smugglers banded together, there were many small vessels which 'ventured a run'. Typical of these was the *Sarah and Grisell* of Perth, a forty feet long craft of thirty-two tons, which in 1724 stood off Robin Hood's Bay and hailed the local fishermen. Someone who watched casks of spirits being sold over the ship's side informed the customs. When the little craft put into Whitby that evening, she was seized, though not without a struggle. When customs officers boarded her, the master and crew attempted to get her underway, and were sailing her out of the harbour until she grounded and a sturdy revenue man knocked out the rudder pin. The master protested that he had put in for provisions on his way to Bergen from France. Underneath his cargo of salt were found over 150 tubs of brandy, but he claimed this to be part of his genuine cargo. It was common for smuggling captains to get a bill of lading for Bergen and, on their way up the east coast of England, put in to land it. If caught near a port they claimed that bad weather had delayed them and run them short of water and provisions. Before many years had passed, stealth and concealment had given way to open beach landings by fast well-armed cutters, frequently in numbers.

In the May of 1777 the previously mentioned Revenue cutter *Swallow* again fell in with the *Kent*, and Captain Mitchell recorded sadly: 'The smuggler would not let us come near to him.' A few days later *Swallow* saw

The Bolts

'… one route by which men fled to escape the
Press Gang and Excisemen'.

the smuggler at Runswick Bay, but was driven off by her guns. During that day *Swallow* chased a small boat with fourteen men in her, thought to belong to *Kent*. Even the small arms fire from the small craft was heavy enough to keep the government men off. In the September of the same year, *Swallow* again figures in customs' records. She hailed a cutter at sea, but as it was dark, anchored off Saltburn. At dawn, the cutter charged *Swallow* under full sail, striking her on the quarter, and the skipper threatened Mitchell with sinking, if she did not leave the anchorage. Once again poor *Swallow* was driven away, but she was probably less than half the size of some of the smuggling craft. In 1787, the biggest Customs cruiser was *Repulse* at Colchester, of 210 tons and a crew of thirty-three men. *Mermaid*, at Newcastle, was only 112 tons, and had only ten guns and thirty men. *Swallow* had only twenty-four crew, and presumably smaller tonnage than *Mermaid*.

Smuggling craft came in all shapes and sizes, but among the biggest was a 250 ton Plymouth built vessel with 100 crew. If others were smaller, all were built for speed. The cutter was the favourite craft, with her immense sail area. She had only a single mast, but often an extra long running bowsprit to carry a big foresail.

Compared to the glittering rewards of smuggling, pay in the Customs cruisers was dismally low. About the time of the incidents just recounted, captains of Customs Board cruisers were paid £50 a year, and chief mates not more than £35. A deck-hand on a smuggling vessel could earn as much in half a dozen trips across the North Sea. Even a labourer could match it with a dozen nights tub-carrying. By 1810 the cruiser commanders were only paid £100, but in that year were given a long awaited rise to £250. Any prize money the captains gained by capturing smugglers was hard earned.

The smugglers did not always have their own way. *Kent*, despite her sharp teeth, was captured off the Yorkshire coast. Two Excise cutters and two Royal Navy vessels had chased the smuggler out of Bridlington Bay on July 7th, 1777. On the day following, *Pelican*, and *Arethusa* — another naval frigate, were sailing northwards. Southwards from Robin Hood's Bay sailed the two Excise cutters. When the latter were still some way off Filey, they hailed *Kent* and the schooner captain shouted: 'Fire, you . . . . and be damned to you!' The big schooner then beat to quarter and for an hour the three vessels fired continually. Finally the two frigates came up from the south and the battle was over. The schooner used her sweeps to try and outsail the frigates, but was overhauled, her main mast shot through.

'Stoney', whose real name was George Fagg, an outlawed criminal, was captured, and *Kent's* sailing master and four of her crew were killed. The rest of the smuggling crew of thirty-nine were put aboard the naval frigate *Arethusa,* and the two Customs cruisers took the *Kent* into Hull, where her guns and ammunition were taken ashore and put in the King's warehouse. The schooner was armed with sixteen four-pounders, and twenty swivel guns, also having a big stock of gunpowder, blunder-busses and muskets. Her cargo was 1,974 half anker tubs of spirits (or almost 8,000 gallons), and 554 oilskin bags of tea. She had been built at Folkestone, another famous home of smugglers, and specially rigged for fast sailing, her mainmast being seventy-seven feet tall, and her mainboom fifty-seven feet long. Excluding her cargo, ship and tackle were assessed at £1,405, so she was a fair prize. Among the prisoners were those suspected of murdering a soldier while he was helping a Whitby customs officer the year before. There was £100 reward on their heads. Later a man named Richard Curtis stood trial and was found not guilty of murdering the dragoon. For his smuggling crimes, he was impressed into a naval man-of-war.

The following year another notorious Robin Hood's Bay smuggler was captured. It was in 1774 that the Excise craft *Mermaid* and *Eagle* had been chased out of the bay. One of the smuggling skippers on that occasion was a lurid character known as 'Smoker' Browning. His real name was David Browning and for many years it had brought an angry curse to the lips of most customs officers of the North East. At that time his vessel was a large well-armed shallop, named *Porcupine,* of Sandwich. His nick-name, 'Smoker', occurs in the Sussex area around this period.

'Smoker' was sighted in the North Sea in 1777 by Captain Mitchell of the *Swallow,* this time in a cutter of about 130 tons with a crew of about forty. In his report Mitchell says: 'Smoker waved us to keep off.' The smuggler had fourteen carriage guns, and four three-pounders, as well as a great number of swivel guns. (Swivel guns were small pieces mounted to fire down into an open boat. They often fired stones as well as iron shot). In 1788, Captain Whitehead of the Excise cutter *Eagle,* from Newcastle, saw the smuggling cutter and chased her a mile or two north of Robin Hood's Bay. On being hailed, the smugglers fired a volley with their muskets, wounding one of *Eagle's* crew, and followed this with a fusillade from their swivel guns. Captain Whitehead 'thought it prudent to get away from her as fast as he could, the greatest part of his people having quitted the deck.' For an hour the smuggler chased *Eagle,* firing the whole time. The vessel's master was 'Smoker' Browning, *Eagle's* old enemy, who on this occasion put twenty shot through her sails, shot away her mizzen rigging, and put more shot in two masts and her boat. Captaining a customs cruiser was no sinecure! Throughout the whole chase, *Eagle's* crew, who knew Browning's voice well, could hear him bawling threats and curses at them.

About this time, the Collector of Hull, a customs official, wrote to the Customs Board in London, saying that a big lugger had been seen off Whitby and described her as 'greatly an overmatch for any of the Revenue cruisers or even for a joint attack on two of them.' He noted that as long as she and Browning's armed cutter 'continued so daringly to insult the coast' there was little prospect of success. Success in capturing Browning was not, however, far distant. On July 15th, 1788, a midshipman on *HMS Kite,* a naval cutter sailing from Beachy Head to the west, sighted a lugger punching her way through the waves with the extra help of a jib sail on a running bowsprit. It was her extra rig that made the midshipman suspicious. He reported to his captain and the cutter swung into the chase. The lugger was fast, but *Kite* was slightly faster. It took four hours to narrow the gap sufficiently for *Kite* to fire her swivel guns and muskets and bring the lugger to surrender. The midshipman who sighted her was sent across and the lugger's skipper brought to *Kite.* He was David 'Smoker' Browning. Asked for his papers, he could only produce a bill of sale. He was bound for Flushing for a contraband cargo, he admitted, adding that only a navigation error had sent him so close to the land. The lugger, which had six carriage guns mounted on deck, was taken to Spithead, and Browning was taken to Chichester for trial and subsequent conviction. Mostly the smugglers escaped the law. On this occasion Browning, a daring seaman, had been betrayed by a simple matter of arithmetic.

The great sea-faring epoch of smuggling was matched by the exploits of the land smugglers. Many Fylingdales families were in league with the free-traders. The architects of the vast enterprise would remain largely anonymous in their yeomen's farmhouses, content merely to finance the operations, but distribution of the contraband needed large numbers of people. To carry the goods, the land smugglers had packs of ponies. These would draw carts or carry fish panniers by day, and kegs of Dutch gin and French brandy by night. Many of the old stables have disappeared from the village, but a number can still be seen. If the schooners or luggers were too big to run their noses on to the beach, the fishing cobles might be used to ferry the goods to the shore. Larger smuggling craft carried their own 'tub-boats', deep heavy craft. A 200 ton schooner like the *Kent* could carry up to 2,000 half-ankers, and several tons of tea made up in hundreds of oilskin bags. An anker was about nine gallons, but a half-size was more convenient for handling. Such a cargo might need over 100 men to handle it. Is it credible then, that these vast enterprises went unnoticed by the authorities?

Some of the landsmen were extremely violent. In the Cleveland area, a few miles to the north, smuggling had reached such a peak by the 1770s that the villagers were in constant fear of their lives. The smugglers set fire to farms, slaughtered cattle, and kidnapped women. During this time of terror, North Riding revenue officers wanted sixty-four dragoons to help them, but none could be spared. A preventive system had been in force since 1674, but 100 years later had evolved only into a system whereby the Excise cruisers guarded the coast as well as they were able, and men known as riding officers kept a vigil of sorts on vast coastal stretches, aided periodically by the army. Later, a water-guard was formed, and at one time a long-boat was kept at the old coastguard station at Wayfoot.

When outsiders ventured into the old fishing village, they took their lives in their hands. Bay wives poured boiling water on to the heads of visiting customs men from their bedroom windows above the narrow alleys. In 1795 the Whitby customs officers desired the arrest of a desperate character known as David Pinkney, of Baytown. But the Whitby office had to record:

> 'We are sorry this has not been executed. This we cannot help, attributing to the irresolution of the Constable of Robinhoodstown where Pinkney resides. The latter, on the approach of the officers, fastened the door of his dwelling house which the Constable at first doubted the power of the warrant to authorise him to break open. He afterwards refused to take that step on the grounds that his life would be endangered from the desperate character of the defendant.'

Without the help of the dragoons, arrests were hard to effect.

Frequently a preventive man was in league with the smugglers. In the March of 1773, for example, the Whitby Customs Collector wrote the following letter to John Robinson, Riding Officer at Robin Hood's Bay:

> 'A great smuggling at Robinhoodstown which had been laid before the Board and by their order sent down here and directed as strict enquiry and full report thereon. As you and Mr Forster are represented to be

greatly concerned therein you are therefore to make a full reply in regard to the smuggling trade at Robin Hood's Bay and also what is alleged against you for concerning, encouraging and receiving gratification for permitting the pernicious trade, as soon as you possibly can that the affair may be speedily laid before the Board.'

Generations of sturdy fishermen and Fylingdales farm hands earned their guineas for a night's work. Those who staggered knee-deep in water with a seventy-pound keg in their arms were catspaws, as often were the captains and the seamen. The men behind the smugglers were more often in the big houses, rather than the small cottages. Syndicates of the well-to-do put up the money. Often a respectable yeoman, parading on Sunday in fine linen and burnished boots, was the man who listened with most satisfaction to the scuffling of ponies as they wound their way in the dark up to the moorland, heavily laden.

In this connection is believed to have originated the local legend of 'Linger's ghost'. Even at the same time of writing, there are one or two elderly people who will say with a smile: 'I'll not be out tonight — Linger's ghost will be riding.' The saying had its origins in the fact that the said ghost was only observed when a pony train crossed the moor along the old Robin Hood's Bay road. The apparition was a white rider on a white horse. Its mission, considering that the farmer at Linger's Toft, near Thorpe, was known to have returned home in the early hours, carrying a white sheet, was evidently to scare the simple cottagers into locking their doors and minding their own business!

The ringleaders of the smugglers at the Bay remain largely anonymous, though a local historian earlier this century looked with suspicion on two large houses in the district, Thorpe Hall and Raven Hall. At least one celebrated smuggling fraternity on the North Yorkshire coast had a number of gentry and clergy among its members. About the beginning of the 19th century the Whitby customs wrote to a correspondent:

'We yesterday received your letter informing us that you had undoubted intelligence of Sir Charles Turner having declared at his own table that he had procured claret from Guernsey at the low price of 1s 6d a bottle and offering to accommodate his friends at the same rate.'

The story was already the talk of Whitby. The customs man concluded:

'We evidently coincide with you that all possible means should be used to bring such a delinquent to public shame at least for his being concerned in so infamous a transaction.'

Those who made a fortune out of smuggling might later turn a stern face against their old trade. There is a traditional local story of an ex-smuggler of Robin Hood's Bay who refused to let his daughter Alice marry a poor local fisher lad. The young man went to sea to seek his own fortune, swearing he would not return until he found it. Years later, Alice died, being buried in the old Bay churchyard. When her lover returned on the funeral day he hid behind a wall and when the mourners had gone he persuaded the sexton to uncover the coffin and prise open the lid. He kissed the cold lips, and thrusting all the gold coins he had in his pockets into the sexton's pockets, he ran off and was never seen again. According to the old story, contained in a letter, the sexton never spent any of the money, and confessed the matter to a priest on his death-bed.

Legends about the old smuggling days are numerous, but remaining links with the old days very few. Occasionally the writer has heard hints that local families had jealously guarded souvenirs of the freetraders, such as letters from Bay seamen held for smuggling in Cardiff jail, or a coded message in the form of an embroidered handkerchief, and bottles of spirit and rolls of silk discovered in secret cavities. But if this is true, then the owners of these souvenirs keep their ancestral associations with smugglers a secret. The older Bay folk are notoriously 'close' as we say in the North. This reluctance to own any links with smuggling contrasted with the eagerness of a Scarborough man to acquaint anyone interested with the histories of his great grandfathers. Both were smugglers, one being shot and killed by a fellow-smuggler, and the other being the leader of a notorious Cleveland gang which owned their own fast lugger, the *Morgan Rattler*. This informant confessed with a twinkle in his eye that he himself had spent a lifetime in the Inland Revenue, so at least one smuggler's debt to society has been paid by a later generation!

Smuggling went on in most coastal villages in North Yorkshire, but activities at Robin Hood's Bay were the district's biggest headache for the Whitby Excisemen. When, in 1775, a Major of Dragoons at York asked where he was to station an NCO and sixteen soldiers, as directed by the War Office in order to help put down smuggling, the reply from Whitby was most revealing. The customs men thoughtfully allocated the party as follows: two dragoons at Sandsend, two at Hinderwell, another two at Runswick and four at Staithes. But the largest party — the remaining six men, plus the NCO in charge — were all to be stationed at Robin Hood's Bay. Thirty years later, the Army was still being asked to help the revenue men. In November, 1809, the Whitby Collector wrote to Lieutenant General Pye, at Beverley:

'I beg leave to inform you in answer thereto that the towns of Robin Hood's Bay and Staithes are general rendezvous for large vessels such as cutters and luggers employed in smuggling. They generally make use of one of these places when they first come on the coast and where the principal agents reside who direct this illicit traffick. On the arrival or the expected arrival of the smuggling vessels the agent sends, immediately, secret notice thereof round the country to the different people concerned in smuggling who assemble at the landing places pointed out to them in great numbers. As soon as the smuggling vessels arrive at the rendezvous the cargo is either brought on shore by their own boats assisted by the fishing cobles or is turned away along the coast by these cobles to some more convenient landing places where a large proportion of the smuggled goods is taken immediately into the interior of the country by the people by the numerous footpaths that the adjoining moors and hilly country afford.

The remainder is secreted until an opportunity offers of disposing of it in small quantities among the inhabitants of the towns and villages along this coast and I am well afraid that every facility is given the smugglers by almost all the lower class of people and I am sorry to add by a large proportion of the highest ranks of society in this part of the country. I take the liberty of offering my opinion as to the mode to be adopted for preventing this illicit practice. I should recommend strong detachments of infantry stationed at the towns of Robin Hood's Bay and Staithes to be each commanded by a commissioned officer (perhaps a captain, two subalterns and one or more additional trusty NCOs would give more effect to this measure) and that as soon as any of the smuggling vessels appear on the coast, the officer or trusty NCO with a party attended by officers of this revenue should, as acquainted with the different by-roads, be each sent to landing places.'

The Exciseman cannot have held too high an opinion of the aid he was likely to receive from this substantial military establishment. He suggests

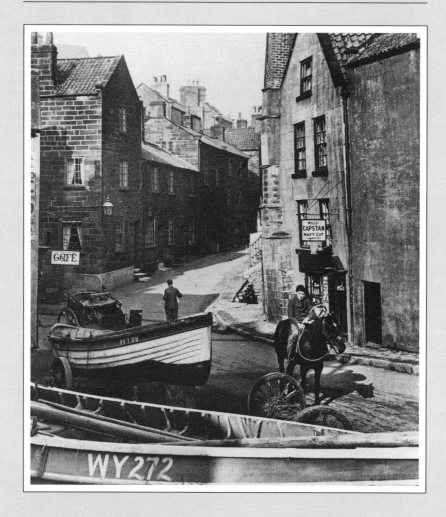

The Former Fishermans Arms (on the right)

'The customs officers were the victors … and …
decided to celebrate.
When dawn broke they were still in the cellar
but both cargo and smugglers were miles away'.

The Nag's Head Inn

'The wounded from the lugger were taken to
the old Nag's Head Inn,
and were supposed to have escaped via a secret passage'.

that detachments of soldiers should be changed often to prevent too friendly relations between them and the villagers, observing: 'I am well aware that every species of temptation will be thrown out to them to induce them to neglect their duty.'

It is doubtful whether military measures alone ever put down smuggling at this bay. Dragoons were still stationed in the village in 1830. They were complaining, in that year, that the shocking state of the local roads was making pursuit of the smugglers very difficult. When things were quiet, Excisemen were allowed to roam through the cobbled alleys unmolested. Here is the record of an official visit by Horatio Roberts, Waiter and Searcher, one winter's evening in 1772:

> 'Went to the house of William Cobb in Robinhoodstown about four in the evening. In a lodging room below stairs upon a bed where Cobb and his wife usually lay, found two and a half anchors of Geneva (gin) and in which same bed four bags of tea, and in the same room in another place, fourteen bags of tea, and in an unlock'd door drawer in the next room, six cannisters of tea, and upstairs at the same time in the said house in an open closet (entered with Excise for sale of spirituous liquors) five bags of tea, and in an adjoining chamber in an open closet twelve cannisters and ten single pounds papers tea. Cobb himself was at home when the seizure was made and his wife told the officer she was privy to the goods being lodged there.'

If the smugglers had a run on, or distribution of contraband was in full swing, the customs men had better beware. Sometimes the clashes were fierce on land as well as on the water. On October 6th, 1779, Excisemen seized 200 casks of brandy and gin, fifteen bags of tea, and a chest full of blunderbusses and cartridges for twenty men. The seizure was only temporary, as the Bay men fought them to surrender everything but twenty of the casks and ten bags of tea. The battle was broken up by the arrival off-shore of the vessel *Dover*, whose crew had just broken into the Hartlepools customs house. Crew and landsmen fought the Excisemen to a standstill. Once the Excisemen surprised the smugglers who were delivering their cargo into the cellars of the old *Fishermans Arms* in The Dock The customs officers were the victors, but a curious sequel took place. During the fight, one of the casks sprung a leak, and the law officers unwisely decided to celebrate. When dawn broke they were still in the cellar, but both cargo and smugglers were miles away.

A celebrated story about the village concerns a fight between a smuggling lugger and a government cutter in the first years of the 19th century. A Bay coble put out to rescue the smugglers. It is said that on this evening so many guns were firing that it was possible to read print by the flashes. The wounded from the lugger were taken to the old *Nag's Head Inn,* and were supposed to have escaped via a secret passage. One old whaler, who had a leg blown off, was passed through a house, in by a window at one side, and out of a window at the other. In the village I was told by a lady who is a member of an old shipping family that her great-uncle described the battle to her. He remembered, as a child in 1805, standing at Wayfoot petrified by the explosions, when a man stripped off his coat, thrust it into his arms, and jumped aboard the coble which went to render aid to the crippled lugger.

Distribution of the smuggled goods after they arrived from France or Holland, the Channel Islands, or sometimes possibly from Scandinavia, was a complex job. The village inns would be depots for local sales, and the stream cavern over King's Beck would make a convenient warehouse. On an early 19th century picture of the village, the inn at Wayfoot (on the site of the present *Bay Hotel)* had a gantry overhanging the beach so that at high tide goods could be hauled up from a boat. Inland towns received their contraband via the pony trains which traversed the moorland tracks. A traditional route is the old road climbing up from the bay to Fylingdales Moor. It is shown on larger scale maps as Robin Hood's Bay Road, running across the heather from the junction of the Scarborough Whitby road with the road to Sneaton, via Lilla Howe to Saltergate. It was also known as the Fish Road, and the Salt Road. Fish panniers from Whitby and the Bay, also Runswick and Saltburn, came this way. Under a blue sky it is one of the finest walks in England: eight miles of high moorland, with not one building on the way, and some magnificent views from Lilla Howe, which is the highest point. At times the road sinks into the heather, but the rutted tracks worn centuries ago by the cart wheels never fail to reappear.

At Saltergate was a smith who shod horses for both smugglers and Revenue men. Here also was a coaching house for the stages which ran between Whitby and York from 1788. Saltergate was well connected with the smuggling trade, but its contraband came from the coast and also from inland places, and it was eagerly sought after by Bay fishermen and others. The little hamlet did a roaring trade in salt. In the 18th century there was a tax on salt of 15s a bushel. Villages used considerable quantities for preserving their catches, and the salt was smuggled to the old *Saltersgate Inn*, which dates from about 1650 and was once named *The Waggon and Horses.*

Many a good Robin Hood's Bay wife walked the old Fish Road, with baskets of fish — and with yards of smuggled silk round her waist. There is a local legend that they also carried pig bladders full of gin under their petticoats, and that once the fish wives were caught at Stoupe Beck by customs men, who pierced the bladders with their sword points. People living on the smugglers' route might find a gift of a small keg tucked under their cottage wall as a reminder to them to forget having heard the pony train clip-clopping by. Old Thorpe Hall reputedly had a stone slab sunk into one of its lawns, with a small chamber beneath to receive a regular tub of gin or brandy.

Some lively anecdotes of the Bay's land smugglers were gathered some years ago by the late J.R. Harrison, of Whitby. He published some of these in the *Yorkshire Weekly Post* of September, 1936. His yarns about the adventures of the villagers are characterstic of the sharp wits and verve which kept smuggling so vigorously alive on this section of the coast for so long. One of the most colourful stories is one in which Bay men tricked the Excisemen, stole their boat, and sold it in Holland!

Pretty Jiddy Vardy once visited friends at High Normanby farm, about one mile from Baytown, and she was questioned by a troop of horse soldiers. That morning there had been a 'run' and obviously someone had informed. When Jiddy asked the soldiers why they were at the farm, and their officer said they were 'waiting for friends' it was obvious these friends were the Excisemen. As casually as she could, Jiddy made her way down to the village to warn the smugglers. But the pony train had not long set off across the moors. The dragoons rode into Robin Hood's Bay followed by preventive men on horseback. They rode on to the beach and towards Stoupe. Jiddy persuaded a farmer to give her a lift on horseback to Evan Howe, their direction taking them parallel to the search party on the beach, but a good mile inland. When they reached the hill, at the junction where the track inland from the beach met another, Jiddy dismounted and lit her lantern. She persuaded the farmer to show a light in his window if the dragoons passed his home, as she was sure they would. Skirting a patch of deep swamp in a wide detour near Jugger Howe Beck, she waited. The farm light flickered. Jiddy swung her lantern high, and shouted, safe on high ground. There was an answering shout from the horsemen, who changed direction and swung towards her over the heather. The ruse had worked. Within a minute the horses were floundering belly-deep in the swamp.

In another yarn, Harrison recorded that three Robin Hood's Bay customs men forwarded this report to their headquarters one day:

> *'Were returning to quarters on duty from Whitby when set upon by a company of Whitby smugglers at Hawsker. Were beaten and bound but escaped and reached quarters at three o'clock in the morning. Did not know the men in the darkness.'*

The people believed that there had been an attempt on their lives by a score of men. In fact only two men were involved. They were James Linskill, who lived in a little cottage with his sister near Stainsacre, and Jonas Chaplow, whose home was in Hawsker village. James was said to have been a very old man when he related the story. But at the time of the incident, both men were of powerful physique, and both their fathers had been pressed into the navy, although they protested exemption as herring fishermen. Neither returned to his home.

Their sons, together with other men, had been engaged in a 'run' at Hawsker Bottoms, half a mile north of Robin Hood's Bay. These two were responsible for getting the goods inland, and at dark their horse sledge set off with a load of gin tubs, two tubs being left at an old shed near Knipe How cross roads. While in the shed, they heard voices, and on looking out were annoyed to see customs men approaching in the pouring rain. The two smugglers prudently shinned up a ladder into the loft and hid in the hay, to wait for the next move. The Excisemen were merely sheltering from the weather, but unfortunately one kicked a tub. One customs man thought there might be contraband hidden in the hay over their heads. He jumped up and caught hold of a beam, but it gave way and he fell back on the floor, injuring himself. At this precise moment, James and Jonas, trying to pick an escape hole in the thatched roof, dislodged some stones which crashed to the ground outside. The customs men dashed from the hut, their clubs at the ready. Said one: 'You go that way round, and I'll go the other.' Seconds later the two smugglers, peeping through the thatch, heard the sound of blows. Dropping down inside the hut, they ignored the customs man lying injured on the floor. Then one of the other two officers came through the door and was felled by Jonas with two blows to the face. The third man the smugglers found outside lying unconscious in the moonlight, knocked on the head by his friend in mistake. They carried him inside. Said James: 'I am sorry to

Oliver Storm c.1915 (on the left)

'The last of the traditional fishermen'.

have to tie you gentlemen, but you will give the alarm before we return to our homes in Whitby.' The three officers pleaded to be allowed to proceed to Robin Hood's Bay, but the smugglers were firm. Only lightly tying them so they would be free within an hour or so, they ran home across the fields. It was James Linskill, incidentally, who was said to have a secret underground chamber at a stable at Spring House Farm, where he worked, and where he stored contraband regularly, unknown to the farmer.

Hiding places, bolt holes and allegedly secret passages abound. It is said that a bale of silk could pass from the bottom of the village to the top without once leaving the houses. This was accomplished by the use of double cupboards. Many of the houses had interior doors leading from one home to another, probably because when a son or daughter married, a tiny garden was sacrificed as the site of another cottage, linked by these doors. When the later occupant of novelist Leo Walmsley's old home in King Street (built in 1620) moved in she found that the wooden back of a first floor landing cupboard was all that separated her home from an adjoining one. Sometimes the houses were connected through the cellars. Two homes in The Dock, one of them the former *Fishermans Arms*, were linked by a properly constructed 'window' in the cellar wall. A similar passage was found in a house in The Square.

Many are the stories of 'secret' passages from the old inns, but whenever one is mentioned it is usually found to connect with the picturesque stream cavern, which is formed by the roofing of the King's Beck for about 150 yards, and dates probably from the 17th century. It hides the stream as it rushes past a shale cliff and disgorges it again at Wayfoot on to the beach. The cavern, which is strongly constructed of stone, is really an elongated bridge. Its purpose was surely to provide more building space on top. No one knows who built it or when, but the old *Fishermans Arms* dates from 1680, and it must pre-date that. The old bridge which carries the main road across the King's Beck probably dates from the early 17th century. There is no mention of a Robin Hood's Bay bridge in the 1589 bridge accounts of the North Riding, nor in the 1616 list. Yet in 1661, at New Malton Quarter Sessions, £30 was ordered to be paid for repairs to the Robin Hood's Bay Bridge. Again, in 1676, at Helmsley Quarter Sessions, £80 was said to be needed for the bridge's repair. At this time, masons were paid 1s a day, so the bridge, and certainly the cavern, were major civil engineering feats for the little community. About this time, judging by the continual complaints to local Sessions Courts, Bay folk were not renowned for keeping their roads and public works in good repair.

Whoever did build the stream cavern, provided a ready-made warren for the smugglers. Many old buildings were once linked with it. One was the *Fishermans Arms*, once the home of the last Bay fisherman, Oliver Storm, and later of his widow. Now this particular cellar is filled in with several feet of solid concrete. There was a linking tunnel with the old *Nag's Head Inn*, now a private house, on the opposite side of the road. Bay children used the old cavern as a playground, and it still holds a few mysteries.

Once inside the Wayfoot entrance, the cavern decreases in height and width after a short distance. About fifty feet from the entrance there is a junction with a second tunnel on the south side, which brings Marna Dale Beck to join King's Beck. In the vicinity of this junction, clearly visible in the wall of the main tunnel, are the ends of passage-ways of varying size. These are now carefully blocked up, and most of them seem to be in the direction of either present-day inns or those of a former period. A few feet inside the entrance, on the right, is a small twelve-inch wide culvert, possibly once leading to the *Bay Hotel*. Further inside, on the left, is a blocked-up passageway which looks as though it was once a substantial opening. Further on still, on the right, is a blocked-up opening about two and a half feet high. This appears roughly underneath the old *Fishermans Arms*. Yet another blocked passage lies in the right hand wall, a little further on. Lastly, still on the right hand side, is similar evidence of an old opening, possibly underneath another former inn.

The offshoot tunnel on the south side of King's Beck is also interesting. A short distance along it is a third and smaller tunnel, leading off at a sharp angle and partly blocked. The roof over the junction of these two branch tunnels is not stone, but beams and boards — part of the flooring of a house. This is the tunnel evidently which once led into the cellar of the former *Nag's Head*. Through this labyrinth, the crew of the smuggling lugger made their escape after the battle with the customs cutter in the first years of the 19th century. Though these old culverts may have provided ingress to smugglers, offering storage for tubs of gin and bags of tea, probably they were built as drainage systems from the old inns, their original purpose being the prosaic one of hygiene. Legend about 'secret tunnels' dies hard however; it was strongly rumoured that the old *Mariners' Inn* in The Square had such a passage, but Mr George Collinson, for many years mine host at the *Bay Hotel*, who was born in the *Mariners'*, had never heard of it. The *Laurel Inn*, on the bend above the bridge, has been mentioned as one building connected with King's Beck by a tunnel, and there is a small culvert under the bridge arch, in direct line with the inn.

Another tunnel strongly believed to have been a hiding place for contraband is about one mile south of the village, near Stoupe Browe. Here there is a tunnel running down to the sloping cliff known as Slam Gutter. About 150 yards long, it is a relic of the old drainage system for the long vanished alum works. Running off this tunnel, which is big enough to walk through, is a second tunnel running underneath the orchard of Stoupe Browe cottage to the house cellar itself. There is the trace of a bricked-up opening in one corner of the latter.

At Low Peak Farm, a little further south along the cliff, there is a curious relic, found half way down the cliff by the farmer, who towed it to the top with his tractor. It is an ancient, and simply fashioned cannon, about eight feet long. It may have been left behind by a smuggling craft, or alternatively may be part of a much older coastal defence scheme.

Whether Bay figured much in any later period of smuggling as the 19th century progressed is doubtful. There are one or two smuggling yarns of comparatively recent date. The daughter of an old seafarer related how the ship masters of the early 1900s, if their ship was passing this part of the coast en route to a home port, would telegraph the arrival date to friends in the village. When the ship passed Ness Point, fishing boats would be out at sea, to collect the goods, returning under the noses of the coastguards, who had been known to inspect incoming craft. Sometimes the ships did not stop. Instead goods would be flung overboard to be picked up by the cobles. A cane chair from Madeira was a favourite article, probably with a bottle or two tied to the wickerwork.

I chatted with an old sea captain who is now dead, and mentioned this anecdote. 'Anything that would float was smuggled in that way', he asserted. At the time we were seated at a table. The old man continued, with a twinkle under his white brows: 'In fact, something in this room was brought ashore for me in old .....'s coble.' He tapped his pipe significantly on the very beautiful antique table on which our elbows rested. Long after his death, an old friend of his told me that this man had taken part in liquor-running to American fishing vessels during the Prohibition period of the 1930s when his owners had closed an eye to his activities during a time when other cargoes were none too numerous. Perhaps this old man was the very last Robin

Hood's Bay smuggler — but only perhaps!

If he was, he operated over a century after the end of the really dramatic days. The armed fleets waging war on the North Sea, backed by wealthy syndicates of landsmen, had to give way eventually. What ended the free-trading, with its daring open beach landings? It was a combination of sterner laws, and more efficient policing of the seas. After the battle of Waterloo, the Government totally freed from crippling wartime burdens for the first time in many years, began to make headway in their fight against the smugglers. For once, the Navy could devote its whole energy to a coastal blockade, and from the 1830s, fast steam vessels overhauled the smugglers' sailing ships effortlessly. Limit laws were enforced mercilessly, and vessels found within a certain distance of the British coast with spirits in less than forty gallon casks were forfeited and broken up. The figure head of a broken up smuggling vessel can still be seen nailed to the wall of a former inn in Baxtergate, Whitby.

The penalties for smuggling grew enormous. In 1827 the Cleveland smuggler John Andrew, of Saltburn, was ordered to pay the impossible sum of £100,000, and kept in York Castle for two years until political influence secured his release. Finally, the reduction in spirit duties had a great effect. The smugglers' profits no longer compensated for the risks they took.

A COMMUNITY OF FISHERFOLK

 he tightly-packed houses of old Baytown were mostly the homes of men who fished the North Sea and roved the world's oceans. From a few humble huts on the cliff, the community multiplied until it reached its fishing peak in the mid-19th century, before the introduction of the trawl, which gradually reduced the inshore fishing fleets. In addition, the keel boat, carrying six or seven crew, became a more economical proposition than the coble, and fishermen left the village for deeper harbours. A few men still go to sea from Robin Hood's Bay, but not in the traditional high-shouldered Yorkshire coble. The fishing industry finally expired in the first years of the Second World War when the last of the traditional fishermen, Oliver Storm, drew up his coble for the last time. There are still one or two families in the parish carrying on a tradition in the Merchant Navy, and a number of retired seafarers have returned to live in Bay.

The story of the Bay fishermen stretches over 1,000 years, and many generations of old salts lie side by side with generations of deep sea mariners in the old churchyard on the hill overlooking the sea. The latter-day inshore fishermen are immortalised in the Walmsley novels, but the author was only just in time to record their lives.

The very first fishermen had settled in the old forests near Raw. Their ancestry was linked closely with the Norsemen. They chose to live a mile or more from the sea for protection against piratical invasion and, like their Viking ancestors, they both fished and farmed. Fishing took place from light craft resembling the old longship, which suited rocky shelving beaches. This family resemblance between the 10th century clinker-built galley, with its dragonesque prow, and the present day coble, is a fascinating one. One may see the coble at several places on the north east coast of England, where it has been developed for landing stern-on at open beaches like Robin Hood's Bay, Staithes and Runswick. One evening as I strolled in a Norwegian fjord, 100 miles from the open sea, I could have sworn I saw one. Not until I took

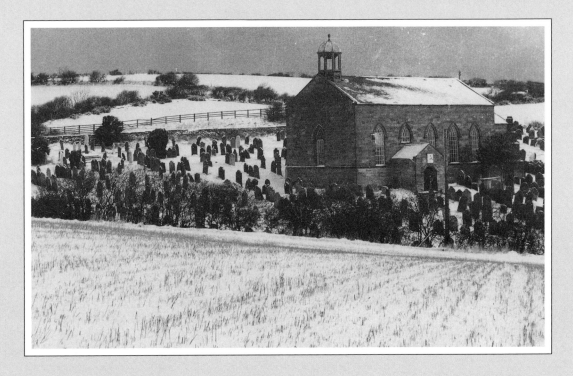

St. Stephen's Church, Raw

'… generations of old salts lie side by side with generations
of deep sea mariners in the old churchyard'.

Bay Cobles

'… surely stemmed from the sure canny eye of the
old Viking boat builders'.

The Coastguards and Lifeboat Crew

'All fishing villages on the coast had their own
distinctive jersey knitting pattern'.

The Shelving Grass Cliff to the South of the Village

a second look at the small fishing boat did I see small differences; but it was so like a coble, with curving strakes, that I might have been looking at one of the Whitby boats. Both this little craft, and those that sailed from Bay, and still sail from other Yorkshire harbours, surely stemmed from the sure canny eye of the old Viking boat builders.

The coble has a high bow to face the surf, both in launching and in making stern-facing landings. The long tiller moves a heavy rudder which both acts as a centre-board and balances the high bow. Though it is a fine sea-boat, the coble nevertheless needs skilful handling in heavy seas. 'Boat and harbour in one' it has been called. Two types of boat were used by Robin Hood's Bay men; a large one about forty feet long, known as a 'plosher', for herring fishing, and a smaller coble about thirty feet long, for winter or line fishing. The latter were generally painted blue, often with a red band on the strakes.

Before the coming of the railway to the district a century ago, men packed their catches in wicker panniers and walked and rode over the rough moorland track to Pickering and York, where they sold their catches and bartered for goods. About 1800 a Bay woman called Molly Baxter would walk to Pickering with a fish basket; small wonder the old Robin Hood's Bay road was also known as the Fish Road, and Old Wives' Trod.

There were twenty boats at the village in King Henry VIII's day. In 1945 there were none. The early 19th century was the peak of the local fishing industry, with as many as 130 regular fishermen sailing thirty-five cobles, as well as five larger herring boats and five lobster boats. The once tiny community had become one of the largest on the north east coast, when Whitby itself had only a handful of fishermen and Scarborough only three large boats. Probably the village's isolation, surrounded on three sides by high moorland only crossed with difficulty, would keep the community socially and industrially intact. Few men would leave to marry elsewhere, and as sons grew old enough to hold an oar they would follow the sea.

Many of the old houses were built between 1650 and 1750, and these would be hard days for the poorer fisherfolk. In 1730 herrings fetched from ten to twenty a penny, and haddocks from 10d to 20d a score. Fishermen did not wax fat on these prices, but a house could be rented from 40s to £5 a year in the Whitby district. Beef and mutton were only 2d per pound, with small chickens at 2d, and butter dear at 4d per pound. At this time local farm workers were paid only 8d a day and board in winter, and up to 1s 6d daily with board in summer.

In the 1800s the village had a great throng of fishwives and their husbands hard at work barrelling fish and mending nets when the boats were drawn up in The Dock, and on the shelving grass cliff south of the village which has now eroded away. On most evenings, a crowd would gather on the beach to help haul up the heavy cobles. The alleys would be full of brown nets drying, and children at play. Fishwives wore canvas petticoats as they worked, and the men donned red and blue jerseys, often with a cap of sealskin, and high heeled boots, or hip length leather sea boots. All fishing villages on the coast had their own distinctive jersey knitting pattern, and the Bay pattern was knitted in moss stitch and small cables. The Flamborough diamond, cable and moss was sometimes used.

By this time, many of the Bay folk owned, through partnerships, cobles and bigger craft. Later they bought ocean going vessels. The fishing industry was simply organised. According to George Young, in his *History of Whitby*, there were five five-man boats of up to fifty eight tons in the bay in 1817. These were worth £600 each, and were at sea from June onwards until Christmas, usually sailing on Monday and returning on Friday. About forty six feet long and sixteen feet broad, they had a draught of over six feet, and were clinker-built and decked, with three masts carrying up to four sails. They also carried two small boats.

The big craft would fish between the coast and the Dogger Bank, the smaller ones being unshipped at sea, using baited lines drawn across the current. On their return, the fish was sold at Whitby or Bay to fishwives, fishmongers and panniersmen. Three times as much wet fish was sold as was barrelled, so most of the catches were probably consumed inland within a reasonable radius of the village. Merchants in Leeds and York also took great quantities of cod, ling, halibut and turbot, and some even went to London later. In August, the herring fishing began, and herring was sold fresh at Whitby and other markets. Usually the big 'ploshers' set out for Yarmouth in the middle of September, and did not return until the beginning of November.

A number of the fishwives went with their men to Yarmouth for the season in the same way as Scots fisher lasses followed their own boats to Yorkshire. On returning from Yarmouth each boat was laid up for the winter and the winter cobles were used until the following March. Partnerships changed in this season from five or six men on the larger boats to three men on each

The National School in the 1890s

Children on the Beach – c.1900

smaller coble. In a good herring season, each boat would net between thirty and sixty lasts (a last is 10,000 herrings) at £7 to £8 a last.

The village industry was geared to include all ages and both men and women. Boys would help to mend nets and make lobster pots. When a man grew too old and stiff to face the long cold hours in the cobles, he would change to lobster and crab fishing. The older fishermen carried on this type of work both summer and winter with as many as 300 pots used on one boat. The women baited lines, and helped haul up the boats.

Eventually, from owning cobles and shares in larger boats, some wealthier families rose to acquire trading vessels. Men who had saved their earnings from work with the Whitby whaling fleet, or from fishing, would buy a quarter share, then a third or more, in a sailing ship.

In 1867 the old Robin Hood's Bay Mutual Shipping Insurance Company, formed in 1806, insured vessels to the total value of £94,300 — a very large sum for a small Yorkshire village. About that time, 174 ships were owned by Bay men and registered at Whitby. Some of nearly 300 tons were insured for up to £1,700. Many were coal-carrying brigs, but others sailed to the Baltic, the Mediterranean, and as far away as America.

A visitor in 1858 recorded:

> 'The trade in fish has given place to trade in coal; and Bay Town owns about eighty coal brigs and schooners, which sail to Edinburgh, to London, to ports in France, and one, which belongs to a man who a few years ago was a labourer, crosses the ocean to America. There are no such miserable paupers as swarm in the large towns. Except the collier crews, the folk seldom leave the parish, and their farthest travel is to Hartlepool in the steamer which calls in the bay on her way to Scarborough.'

Many of the old Bay mariners could scarcely read or write when they left the village school at an early age; nevertheless they qualified for their mate's and master's tickets. The first school had opened in 1810 in two cottages in The Square, and the National School came into existence in 1814. In 1915 there were a hundred boys and sixty eight girls on the roll. There were also navigation schools in the village — as many as four at one period. Shipowners were bound to give apprentices board and lodging when ships were laid up for overhaul in Whitby, and the youths were made to use their shore leave profitably, being tutored in groups by retired master mariners living in the village.

Collecting Crabs

A Collier Calls at Bay c.1891

Though fisher families rose to owning their own vessels, life on the sailing ships was no sinecure for master or apprentice. Sometimes the Bay-owned schooner or brig might anchor close to Ravenscar and the master rowed ashore for a night in his own home. The son of one of the owner-masters, Mr Fred Mennell, of Robin Hood's Bay, recalled that his father went to sea as apprentice to his own father at twelve, and became a master at nineteen. Mr Mennell's elder brother sailed with his father when only twelve months old and was shipwrecked with him off Cuxhaven in 1858. The captain and his wife managed to get into a boat, the chief mate being in charge of the child. After this the storm grew to such strength that the ship all but disappeared beneath boiling waves, and those who reached land gave up all hope of ever seeing the child again. But when dawn broke, Captain Mennell, scanning the wreck heartbrokenly through his telescope, saw the baby lashed to the rigging, and he was soon rescued, together with the mate.

The sea was a rough master to the men of old Baytown, but their devotion to it never wavered. Tales of the old sailing days, whether beating round the Cape or sailing the lifeboat from Wayfoot in a gale to the rescue of a foundering ship, would fill more than one book, had they been recorded. Whether near or far from home, hundreds of Bay fishermen and seamen lost their lives at sea. Up in the churchyard of old St. Stephen's on the hill many of them lie beneath often undecipherable old gravestones. One inscription which allows no doubt about the deceased's profession says:

> *'Tho Boreas blast and Neptune waves*
> *Hath tossed me to and fro,*
> *By God's decree you plainly see,*
> *I'm harboured here below.*
> *But here I do at anchor ride*
> *With many of our fleet.*
> *And once again I must set sail,*
> *My Saviour Christ to meet.'*

Another notes pathetically:

> *'By storms at sea two sons I lost*
> *Which sore distresses me,*
> *Because I could not have their bones,*
> *To anchor here with me.'*

Visitors on the Beach, 1904

Bay wives feared the sea, with good cause. But in the late 18th and early 19th centuries they had an enemy they feared as much, if not more, than the sea: the Press Gang. This custom was not outlawed until 1883 and the gang were, deservedly, the most hated men on the coast. When they were in the village, the women would beat a drum to warn their men. About 150 years ago a farmer named Mossburn lived in a glen running down to the sea near Bay. His two daughters, Hester and Dorothy, had two local lads, Bill and Peter, as sweethearts. One of them had spurned the advances of another local girl called Polly. This girl, stung by a rebuff, is supposed to have betrayed Bill to the Press Gang, and he was dragged from the farmer's home. His brother and Mossburn went to rescue him, but the unlucky farmer was clubbed unconscious, and the two brothers disappeared. Not a word was heard of them from that night until their return four years later. They were thought lucky to return at all. Both had been badly wounded aboard a man-of-war, and were allowed a discharge. The girl who betrayed them had by this time lost her reason, and wandered about the moors telling people she 'was waiting for her lad to come home from the sea.'

The gang was always busy, for the Admiralty was desperate to fill the gaps in the ranks caused by desertions. Although they risked death, sailors would do so cheerfully to put behind them the bestial conditions in the British Navy of the time, and in 1803 it was estimated that the number of seamen disguised as farm labourers on a ten mile wide strip of the coast between Whitby and the Humber was 1,000. In the latter half of the 18th century the number of seamen in the British Fleet swelled from 50,000 to 129,000. Sailors and fishermen were supposedly exempt, but the Press Gang had a rough and ready interpretation of the rules and one group roamed the Whitby area from its base on the River Tyne. The chances of a young fisherman or farm hand returning to the village were not high. Before about 1800 a million navymen and seamen had died from scurvy alone. Living conditions aboard the old ships were a nightmare, and disease was prevalent. Apart from anything else, many ships fell apart because they were made from unseasoned timber, and many foundered.

The Press Gang did not always have their own way in the Whitby area. Two naval lieutenants brought a gang from Tyneside one night in 1793, intending to tour the coastal villages, including Bay. They billeted themselves in a Whitby house, but about 7.30 in the evening a crowd of up to 1,000, many of them women, packed the street and stoned the windows. One account says that by nine that evening, several of the Press Gang had been wounded, and the mob finally broke down the door. They beat the naval officers and their men with such savagery that 'only the arrival of a troop of armed soldiers prevented the house from being burned down.' When the Gang were at Bay, the beat of the warning drum would set women weeping and men scurrying between the houses in the narrow streets.

The sea claimed most of the victims of sudden death. One of the earliest recorded sea tragedies was that of August 6th, 1686, when six fishermen were lost in their boat at Stoupe Brow. They included Robert Moorsom, Thomas Storm senior, Thomas Storm junior, Thomas Robson and John Skerry. In the April of that year Thomas Allatson and Robert Farside, gentlemen, together with a Scots guest named Alexander, were drowned in an attempt to save life at a shipwreck. In 1690 five Bay men were drowned in their boat near Fylabridge, which may be Filey Brigg. They were Thomas Storme (master), Robert Storme, Bartholomew Storme, James Holme and Robert Staincliffe. Of the twenty five men from Bay who were lost at sea between 1686 and 1784, twelve were Storms. Out of the 261 names of drowned seamen recorded by Mr William Conyers the Storms numbered forty three. The last Storm to lose his life at sea was thought to be William Storm, MM, who died in the Second World War.

Edward Storm, Master Mariner, RN, died of yellow fever at Antigua in 1784. John Knaggs died at Batavia in 1829. The boy Jelson Carnforth went down with his barque *Heart of Oak* off Gibraltar in 1865. Reuben Storm perished with the *Ville de Paris* in 1782 while in charge of French prisoners. Thomas Rickenson died at Port Royal. Henry Keld was lost in the Bay of Bengal in 1852 ... the register of missing seamen is tragically long for the size of the village. Some of its most honoured names are the Bay lifeboat men who drowned within sight of their own homes. On one winter's day in 1843 six Bay fishermen lost their lives. The lifeboat had capsized on its way to a wrecked brig, being struck by a heavy sea, and four of its crew drowned. On seeing this, five more Bay men put off in a second boat, but this also overturned, and two of the five lost their lives. Thanks to the lifeboatmen of Bay, ninety one lives were rescued between 1881 (when the R.N.L.I. took over the running of the lifeboat) and 1931 (when the lifeboat station closed). Many more lives were probably saved by the local lifeboat between 1830 and 1881. The lifeboat house still stands on its commanding site opposite Wayfoot, but it now has a new role. Most visitors hardly give it a second glance!

**The Second Robin Hood's Bay R.N.L.I. Lifeboat,
the Mary Ann Lockwood, 1902 – 1931**

The Robin Hood's Bay Lifeboat, c.1920

No mention of the lifeboat service could be made that did not include the epic rescue of the crew of the brig *Visitor* on January 19th, 1881. This was the famous occasion when the Whitby lifeboat was brought to Bay by road, and the year when the forty years old Bay boat was replaced by a new self-righting one. At the time of the rescue, a blizzard raged and there were heavy seas. Bay men dug their way through deep snow drifts with Whitby helpers while the lifeboat *Robert Whitworth* was dragged by eighteen horses from Church Street, Whitby, to Bay Bank top. It was a maddeningly slow march against time while the screaming wind and waves smashed the little wooden brig.

The *Visitor* was a vessel of 209 tons, and had sixteen joint owners, no uncommon feature of the times, one of them being Trueman Robinson of Robin Hood's Bay. With Captain Anderson and five hands she had left Shields for London on January 16th, 1881, but close to Flamborough Head at 4 p.m. the wind changed and began to blow from the east with snow. All the sails were blown away by the gale except the main topsail and main staysail. The ship was driven north, and at 2 a.m. on the 19th she anchored off Bay. One report said she was four miles from the shore. At 8 a.m. the *Visitor* foundered with five feet of water in her hold, and the crew took to their long boat. The lifeboat was lowered down the steep street by ropes, and launched. The waves were too mountainous for it, and it was forced to return, with some oars smashed to matchwood. An argument had taken place about which place to launch the boat. The Whitby men wanted to go straight in at The Dock, but local men counselled the use of the landing 200 yards away, where there was a narrow stretch of sand between two rocky reefs. Finally, a Bay man, John Skelton, in a lull of the wind, waded and swam towards the wreck, plotting a safe course for the lifeboat to follow, and the brig's crew were brought to safety. That day was the Congregational bazaar, and the Shepherd's Walk, so both rescued and rescuers were easily fed. The Shepherd's Walk, incidentally, was the ceremony of the local Lodge of the Loyal Order of Ancient Shepherds, a form of friendly society which helped those who fell upon hard times. Wearing colourful sashes and carrying crooks, the fishermen walked to church and chapel headed by a band, and their anniversary dinner was regarded as one of the outstanding functions of the year.

Many wrecks were thought to be due to the ironstone in the reef which runs a mile out to sea from near Ravenscar. It was supposed to swing the ship's compass, and was often referred to at Board of Trade inquiries. On

The Shepherd's Walk

'Wearing colourful sashes and carrying crooks,
the fishermen walked to church and chapel
headed by a band'.

January 26th, 1860, ten light vessels went aground inside Ness Point, and at least two were wrecked. As many as twenty three carpenters were called in to patch up the rest and refloat them. Three that were salvaged brought £700.

Life at Bay village was not all storms and hard work. The fisher families, despite their isolation, enjoyed the benefits of a closely knit communal life. For a neat word-picture of the village and its people in 1858, there is an account by the itinerant Mr Walter White in *A Month in Yorkshire*:

> *'"Yer master wants ye", said a messenger to a young fellow who sat smoking his pipe in the King's Head, while Martha the hostess fried a chop for my dinner. "Tell him I isn't here; I isn't a-cooming" was the answer, with a touch of Yorkshire which I heard frequently afterwards. From the talk that went on I gathered that Bay Town likes to amuse itself as well as other places. All through the past winter a ball or dance had been held nearly every evening, in the large rooms which it appears are found somewhere belonging to the very unpretending public houses.*

> *On the other hand church and chapel are well attended and the singing is hearty. Weddings and funerals are made the occasion of festivals, and great is the number of guests. Martha assured me that two hundred people were invited when her father was buried, and even for a child, the number will be forty or fifty; and all get something to eat and drink. It was commonly said in the neighbourhood that the head of a Bay Town funeral procession would be at the church before the tail had left the house. The church is nearly a mile away.*

> *A clannish feeling prevails. Any lad who should choose to wed with an outsider would be disgraced. Ourselves to ourselves is the rule. On their way home from the church, the young couples are beset by invitations to drink at door after door, as they pass, and jugs of strong liquor are bravely drained, and all the 1,800 inhabitants share in the gladness. Hence the perpetuation of Todds and Poads. However, as regards names, the most numerous which I saw were Grainger and Bedlington, or Bettleton, as the natives call it.'*

To White's account of funerals it must be added that there were other funeral and wedding customs in the community. On the death of a villager, a neighbour known as the 'bidder' toured the area issuing official verbal invitations. The most honoured were those 'bidden' to be bearers — 'a last token of affection considered highly honourable', says the recorder of a late vicar's notes. Those invited went to the house and, beginning at 10 a.m., dropped in until the hour fixed for a start, being fed in relays all day. 'Not to be bidden was an unforgiveable offence and remained as a grudge for years.' One old Bay man summed up the general attitude to being bidden as: 'If Ah bean't bodden, an' ti t' teate, Ah issent ganning.'

The funeral procession must not travel any way other than the church road. If another path were taken, the dead were provoked, and had the power to 'come again'. Among the Scandinavian people there was talk of a 'hell way' and the dangers attending the dead on their journeys were carefully kept in mind. The fishing families being almost daily nearer to sudden death than the rest of society, were mostly extremely religious, and also held deeply ingrained superstitions. It was said the old fishermen would not take a boat to sea if they met a woman or a pig on their way to the slipway in the morning. And Castle Chambers, on the cliff, was said to be haunted by a witch named 'Nan' who appeared to godless fishermen who pursued their calling on the Sabbath. She was supposed to be seen running up and down the cliff as a cat.

Wedding parties were gay and rumbustious. One custom was the race by village lads to the bride's house to see who would be first to nail her garter to the door. On the way from the church the bridal party would be offered refreshments at several doors and thus the party spirit would be well generated, and also imbibed early in the day.

It was in this early part of the 19th century that Bay was beginning to attract attention from outside. Enforcedly insular due to the lack of proper roads in the district, and the absence of a railway station until 1885, the village neither cared for visitors nor wanted them. A writer in the *Scarborough Repository* of August, 1824, said:

> '*Other popular places which fill up the rides of our visitants are Whitby and its venerable Abbey ruins, and Robin Hood's Bay and its grotesque buildings. These continue to engross the public attention and command a visit.*'

The ratio of deep-sea sailors to inshore fishermen was gradually reversing until, by the First World War, there were only two families fishing from the village, the Storms and the Dukes, and the latter had come from Bridlington and were to leave for Whitby after not so many years. Failing accidents, Bay fishermen were usually long lived. Oliver Storm's widow, recalling her father-in-law, Isaac Storm, who fished with his sons at ninety, said: 'It seemed a shame when he died; there was nothing wrong with him.' He was ninety five or ninety six all the same. One of the Storm patriarchs used to joke: 'We're furriners, for all we're Bay folk.' Most of the family took their remote Scandinavian ancestry for granted. Descendants of the Storm family can be found in this and many parts of both North and East Yorkshire. It is thought they may have originated from the Sturm family of southern Norway's coastal area.

Mrs. Oliver Storm came to the village from Northallerton as a young bride of twenty, and in the 1880s was reputed to be the fastest woman in the village at baiting a line. Baited lines were always used, except for herring and salmon (sea trout) for which the nets were used. Lines were baited with 'flithers' or limpets, alternately with mussels. Often a coble would sail from the bay to Middlesbrough to fetch back the bait. One old Bay man, who was not a sailor, remembered ruefully the day when as a youth he was prevailed upon to take the sea trip to Middlesbrough. After the wind died to a flat calm, he had to help row the heavy boat all of forty miles back again!

Oliver Storm, who died in 1953, was the last lifeboat cox of Robin Hood's Bay. He coxed the *Mary Ann Lockwood* for five years, and his widow had not forgotten, thirty years later, the fear she knew when the boat stood on its ends to meet the North Sea breakers. The men knew fear, too, she said, but they had confidence in her husband. 'All the men would go with Oliver', she recalled proudly.

One important duty the fisherwives undertook was to warn their men fishing off the coast when there was a heavy swell on The Landing — that narrow spit of sand stretching between the scaurs which, before the last war, was marked by posts. A swell by day would send one of the women scurrying up the hill behind the village with a red flag or tablecloth, and when the boats came in, they would either try to land at a cutting in the cliff known as the 'Grinnick' or 'Gunny-hole' or, if the sea was too rough, would stand off for several hours if necessary. By a happy coincidence, one of the leading fishing families lived in a house which stood high on the south bank of the ravine in which the township is built, and its attic window was in line with the run-in to The Landing. If the men were due to land in the dark but the swell was dangerous, an oil lamp would be placed behind a red blind to warn them.

The village still clings to the ways of the sea. Occasionally a local man will take a boat out for lobster or salmon. But the economics of inshore fishing have often defeated those wanting a full-time living. Nevertheless, from time to time, someone will attempt to do so. Small craft lying in The Dock are more likely to belong to weekend sailors. But often they too indulge in an hour or two's pleasure fishing, or launch to help in some minor rescue when the swift tide cuts off unwary walkers on the beach.

A few families follow the sea in the Merchant Navy, preserving old links. Occasionally the talk in the *Bay Hotel,* on the shore's edge, turns to far-off places, and for a moment there is a faint echo of far-off days. It used to be said that on any day one cared to choose, there was a Bay man in every major port in the world. Even over 20 years ago when two Bay men met in the Persian Gulf, while their ships made brief contact there, this was so unusual as to make front page news in the *Whitby Gazette.*

BUILDINGS GREAT AND SMALL

o far this story has been concerned with the village by the sea, its people, and the topography of the dale. Into it must now be drawn the great houses of Fylingdales. Modest in one sense, they nevertheless exerted a powerful influence on the community, and one owner of the old manor house played a key part in an act which was to alter the course of British history.

Whitby Abbey was the first great house to play a large part in local history. Next in importance was undoubtedly Fyling Old Hall, the one time grange of the Abbot of Whitby. There is Thorpe Hall, and a yeoman type farm known as Farsyde House. Two other houses of interest are Fyling Hall, now a private school, and Boggle Hole Youth Hostel, which was a water mill for two and a half centuries at least. The houses of worship in Fylingdales also have interesting histories.

The history of the secular houses has a living link in the centuries old Court Leet of the Manor of Fyling. This meets each December at Bay to discuss common garths, fences and boundaries: it has its own Seneschal, a foreman, moorsman, bailiff and affearors, and exercises customary jurisdiction on behalf of the Lord of the Manor, Mr. Frederic Strickland-Constable.

Fyling Old Hall stands about one and a half miles from the old fishing village, and about a mile from the sea, where the railway line crosses Bridge Holme Lane. It is ten minutes' walk from Mill Beck. Once it was the capital mansion, the ancient grange of the Whitby Abbot, and it is supposed to retain fragments of the old wall of his deer park. There are several other traces of this wall nearby. Two of the old house's wings have gone. Buildings once formed a quadrangle around a central courtyard and were entered through a gatehouse on the north. There was a tythe barn, and together with brewhouses, stables and dairy, it would form the far side of the square.

The farmhouse became a purely private residence in the 1960s when it was converted into a home of great character and charm. One of its most attractive features is an upper room reached by a single short flight of stairs from the kitchen, with a medieval fireplace and a small oriel window. This latter room has been known as the 'chapel' but is without much doubt the ancient solar, or withdrawing room, which in the 13th and the 15th centuries was generally built on the upper storey. It was not uncommon for the Lord of the Manor to have his private chapel in the solar, separated from the living quarters by a movable partition. The fireplace is thought by at least one expert to be 15th century.

The first owner of Fyling Old Hall about whom much is known is Sir Hugh Cholmley, who was born in 1600. After the dissolution, Henry VIII sold Fyling to the Earl of Warwick; Sir Edward Yorke owned the land in 1555, and finally the house and its land passed into the hands of Sir Hugh's great-grandfather, Sir Richard Cholmley, whose wife was Margaret Conyers, or Coniers, daughter of another very old Fylingdales family. Robert Coniers lived at Fyling Hall in 1626 and the family is mentioned in the Whitby Abbot's book as being one which performed the rites of the ancient Horngarth ceremony.

Sir Hugh Cholmley was born at Roxby, near Pickering, and came to Whitby when twenty six years old, to live in the Abbey gatehouse. Finding this too small, he moved to Fyling Hall two years later, while he repaired the former house in which his father had lived. It is said that Sir Hugh was glad to leave Fyling Hall because he and his family moved in before repairs were properly finished, and the damp was still on the walls. Not long afterwards he lost his eldest son, Richard, who was only five years old, and moved back to Whitby. The house and demesnes was sold to Sir John Hotham in 1634.

Sir Hugh had a lively career before his death at the age of fifty five. He served in two of the Parliaments of Charles I for Scarborough. When Queen Henrietta landed from Holland with arms, in March, 1643, Charles made Sir Hugh chief commander of all maritime affairs from the Tees to the Bay of Bridlington. Sir Hugh was called 'the father of Whitby' by Charlton the historian. He helped raise £500 for the erection of Whitby piers. He had been educated at Beverley school, and Cambridge University, and was a barrister. A far-seeing man, he sold many tofts and crofts in the Fyling district on 999 year leases. That is why some buyers of Robin Hood's Bay cottages today find their land still on leasehold to the ancient manor.

The Railway Station, Robin Hood's Bay, c.1900

Sir Hugh fought for Charles on Marston Moor, and later held Scarborough Castle during a twelve months long seige. Surrendering on July 22nd, 1645, he was exiled at Rouen until the death of Charles, when he returned after four years and regaining his estates, opened alum works on the south side of the bay. These provided work for many until they closed early in the 18th century. After the death of his wife, Sir Hugh lived on his Kent estate for a further two years before his own death.

Sir Hugh Cholmley's heir, Nathaniel, married Mary Cholmley, a relative. Their grand-daughter Henrietta married Sir William Strickland in 1778. The family of Strickland is an old one from Westmorland, a branch of which settled in Bridlington. One of the family, Sir Thomas de Strickland, carried the banner of St. George at Agincourt. In 1864 the direct line of the Cholmleys came to an end. The Stricklands then became Lords of the Manor of Whitby and remained the owners of Abbey House, Whitby, until the death of Sir Charles William Strickland, the 8th baronet, in 1909. The present Lord of the Manor is thus the descendant of Sir Richard Cholmley of Roxby, who bought Fyling Hall in 1609.

After Sir Hugh, the next owner of Fyling Hall was the ill-fated Sir John Hotham. He ended his life on the executioner's block on Tower Hill, London. Before buying Fyling Hall, in 1634, he had been knighted, and had fought in the Battle of Prague in 1619 as one of the English volunteers. He was Sheriff and MP for Beverley in five parliaments. Unlike Sir Hugh Cholmley, he was on the side of Parliament and figured in the famous incident in 1642 when Charles decided to land Dutch troops at Hull. England was in uproar at this time; Charles wanted arms for his troops, and Hull was one of Britain's three great arsenals. Hotham, who was governor of Hull, was ordered to hold it for Parliament, and when Charles appeared in person on April 23rd, 1642, he knelt in respect, but then ordered his son to shut the gates in the King's face. After a long argument, during which the King unsuccessfully tried to bribe Hotham, the surrounding land was flooded, and the Royal forces had to retreat. Both Hotham and his son were eventually sent to the Tower on suspicion of being anti-Parliament, and executed. Hotham is buried at All Hallows, Barking.

It was the action at Hull, of the owner of Fyling Old Hall which led directly to a great split at Westminster — certainly the only time anyone from the dale had such an impact on the British constitution!

When Parliament upheld Hotham's disobedience to the King, the

Royalist party withdrew from their seats in the House of Commons. Thirty-two peers and sixty MPs joined Charles at York, while those left at Westminster rapidly enrolled the militia. The Civil War was almost at hand. Thus did the old house have its tiny but dramatic connection with British history. The Hotham family held the estate and the hall until the 18th century.

Farsyde House, a farmhouse a little to the south of Bay village, was also the home of a family with an interesting history. The Farsydes, or Farsides, were of Scots origin, and the first John Farside was bow bearer and ranger to the Forest of Pickering, appointed by James I. The date of the building, which stands a few hundred yards from the cliff, is uncertain. The first Farsyde came here in the 16th century from Farside Castle, Midlothian. His grandson, John Farside, lived at Hutton Buscel and married Jane Wilson of Whitby. Their son William married Ursula, daughter of John Marshall, of Fylingdales, in 1652. This couple lived at Farsyde House, and their son John Farside, born in 1661, married Adeline Robinson of Buckton House, near Flamborough, who inherited Thorpe Hall from her aunt Isabella Conyers. The property became one with the Farsyde lands in 1680, the date which is carved over the west doorway at Farside House. The Farsides owned much land on the south side of the King's Beck, and the Cholmleys much of the land on the north side.

Thorpe Hall, in Thorpe village, was rebuilt in 1640. Long before that it was the home of the Conyers family. Here lived the Rev. George Conyers, incumbent of Whitby 1639-54. He was possibly the George Conyers whose baptism was noted in Fyling church records of 1601, and also possibly the man of that name who owned the Robin Hood's Bay mill in 1624. The old house was the scene of a double tragedy in 1962. In the summer of that year, a dental surgeon killed a young woman there, and afterwards committed suicide.

Fyling Hall, again an attractive, stone built house, set in a commanding position on Park Hill, behind Thorpe village, has been a school since 1935. The house was built by the Barry family, who owned extensive estates in Fylingdales about 1800.

Boggle Hole Youth Hostel, well known to thousands of walkers and cyclists, bore the name of Mill House for 250 years. Until 1928 a water-mill was working here, milling flour and cattle feeds, and salting and curing bacon took place. The house stands in a deep cleft in the high cliffs; the mill

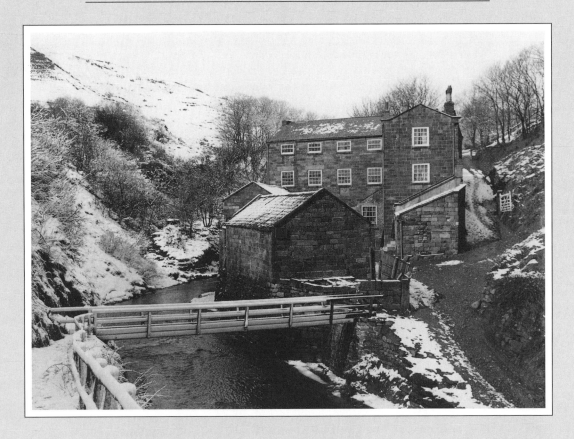

Boggle Hole Youth Hostel

was rebuilt, and new machinery installed in 1839. On the night of August 8th, 1857, a cloud burst caused a great volume of water to rush down Mill Beck. The mill dam behind the house was torn away and the torrent of water undermined and wrecked the house. The housekeeper and a dog were carried away and drowned, but three people in the house managed to escape before the house collapsed. The wrecked house was on the opposite bank of the stream to the mill, and the new house was erected adjoining the mill. In the old days, small ships were 'laid up' on the beach near Mill Beck, and their grain cargoes carried up to the mill to be ground. The house was also an occasional refuge for shipwrecked sailors.

The tower of St. Stephen's Church, Robin Hood's Bay, stands above the new village and is a full one hundred and twenty feet high. The older St. Stephen's, on the hilly road leading to Hawsker, dates from the first years of the 12th Century but was rebuilt in 1821. The first house of worship in Fylingdales was some distance from either, on the moor top, and this was the chapel of St. Ives. At the time of the dissolution it is referred to as St. Iles. Hardly anything is known of its origins, but several factors suggest that it predates the first Norman chapel of St. Stephen's by perhaps centuries.

For two hundred years before the Normans, the area around Whitby may have been virtually churchless due to the ravages of the Scandinavian invaders. The church of St. Stephen's was probably built in 1107 by William de Percy, the Abbot of Whitby. At some time after this there is mention of a church at Saxeby. But where is Saxeby? No one can say for certain, but it is very likely that it is the long-vanished name for the area now known as St. Ives farm. It is only mentioned once in the monks' records.

Alan de Percy, son of the founder of Whitby Abbey, bought land in Fylingdales from Tancred the Fleming, one of the Conqueror's followers who was returning to end his days in his native Flanders. But by a legal quirk, Robert, the son of William of Aketon, or Egton, either as homager or nearest of kin in England and heir at law of Tancred, put in a claim to South Fyling and succeeded. At least he was persuaded by Richard the Abbot to surrender it. His charter granted South Fyling and the church of Saxeby, and all its appurtenances to the monks. The Abbey records are unmistakable: 'Ecclesiam de Saxeby cum omnibus suis pertinentiis.' There is no doubt that a church did exist at this Saxeby, but there is no further mention of Saxeby church. The monks, already possessing a church at North Fyling, on the site where old St. Stephen's now stands, may not have had the need for a second church in the neighbourhood. If it was an Anglo-Saxon chapel, and the very name Saxeby suggests a pre-Norman settlement, it would have suffered from stone-robbers in the centuries between the Danes sacking the district and the Normans arriving.

The name St. Ives or St. Iles very strongly sugests Anglo-Saxon worship. This English saint was known once as Ia, or Hia, an Irish maiden, sister of St. Ercus, who crossed into Cornwall with missionaries and there suffered martyrdom at the mouth of the Hayle river, leaving her name to St. Ives, in Cornwall. She was put to death in the year AD 450. Other evidence for the site of her church in Fylingdales is an enclosure on the moor known as Chapel Garth. Close by this there is a paddock called Peter's Paddock. Not far away is Kirk Moor, and Kirk Moor Gate, both names suggesting the existence of a church. To visit the site of St. Ive's chapel, which is clearly marked on the ordnance survey map for the district, you may take the path from the Scarborough-Whitby road which is about three-quarters of a mile south of the Sneaton junction, to St. Ives Farm, or more pleasurably climb the moor from Fyling Hall. Some 150 years due north of the farmhouse is a grassy dell, really no more than a hollow in the gently sloping ground. One or two stones protrude from the ground still, and the line of the wall's foundation can still be seen.

There is one other reference to St. Ives which is interesting. In 1588, a witness at a local inquiry declared that he had been at divine service in St. Ile's Chapel, and that there was a chapel at Stoupe. A second witness said he thought no service had been performed at St. Stephen's and that one of the chapels was used as a hayhouse and the other a barn. Yet another witness said one of these chapels was called Fyling Hall chapel. Evidently there was more than one building in the district used for religious purposes at the time. Possibly St. Ive's chapel, though long disused, up to that point, was used discreetly again, at a period when religious strife was at its height in Britain, and Elizabeth I had forbidden the saying of Mass in private houses.

Before the Norman monks built their Fyling church in the first years of the 12th century, there was a chapel in the district. The Abbey's founder, William de Percy, granted to the monastery the town of Whitby and the church of St. Mary of Whitby, together with its five chapels, of which Fyling chapel is mentioned as being one. Records say that 'a roof and twenty monks' were put into the Abbey in 1101, half a dozen years before they are thought to have built their new Fyling church on the hill above the bay.

That the original Fyling chapel belonging to St. Mary's of Whitby (which church was built by King Edwin of Mercia), Saxeby church, and the chapel of St. Ives or St. Iles, are one and the same, is beyond doubt.

Little enough is known of the religious life of the dale for the next 500 years. For centuries there was neither endowment nor a parish church for Fylingdales. The chapel of St. Stephen was served by priests direct from the Abbey. In 1353 a visiting archdeacon demanded 7s 6d fee for his visitation, but was tartly informed by Abbot Thomas that he failed to see the necessity: that in fact the church never had had a parson, nor the money to pay for one. After the dissolution a curate was appointed to serve from St. Stephen's. In 1600 his name was John Parsons. In 1685 another curate, John Wilson, stated in the Archbishop's register that there was a house and orchard and the salary was worth £7 6s 8d with an augmentation of £9 13s 4d.

In the period following the Reformation, nonconformity among Fyling folk increased strongly. And by 1614 there was a long list of Catholic objectors known as recusants registered in Fylingdales. In 1651 George Fox, the Quaker, visited Whitby, Malton and Pickering, and in 1668 the Quakers were holding monthly meetings at Fyling, East Raw and Ravens Hill. It was many years before the dissenters had any regular meeting place, the nearest one being at Helmsley.

In the middle of the 18th century, John Wesley came to the Bay several times. On his first visit in 1757 he recorded that he:

> '... rode here from Guisborough, the sixteen miles so called took us between five and six hours riding; so that when I came thither I was quite exhausted ... However, I went to the Key, where a large congregation was waiting and all behaved well, but an honest tar, who was much distressed at my saying "no man is delivered from the fear of death but that he fears God".'

It is thought that the man in question was a smuggler, who took exception to what he thought a slight on his personal courage. The sermon was delivered outside the old waterfront inn. Wesley returned on the following Good Friday, preaching in The Square. He chose the same spot for his sermons in 1766, 1770, 1772 and 1774. The new Wesleyan chapel was built in the year 1779, and Wesley preached there on June 28th. Of his last visit in June 1784, Wesley says:

> 'About one I preached to another congregation of plain people

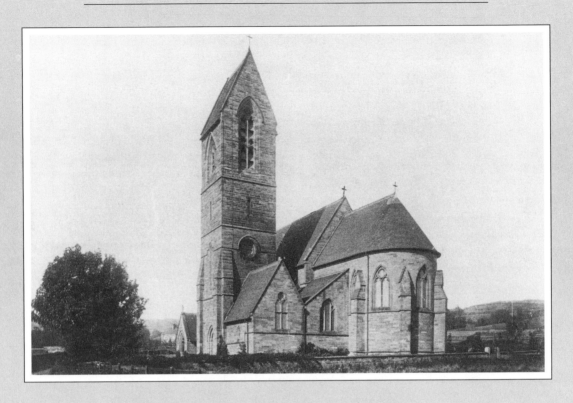

St. Stephen's Church, Robin Hood's Bay

at Robin Hood's Bay. Here was the first society in all these parts, several years before there was any in Whitby; but their continual jars with each other prevented their increase, either in Grace or number. At present they seem to be all at peace.'

A Whitby guide of 1828 speaks of a 'commodious new church' standing on the brow of the hill about one mile from the town, but owing to the Methodist chapel being situated in the town, the inhabitants finding it 'more convenient' to attend public worship there. Old St. Stephen's had had to be rebuilt because in 1816 it was dangerously decrepit, and the anxious parishioners needed £885 to repair it. Because of its outlying position a new church nearer the township would seem to have been the proper answer, but it was not until over fifty years later that building one began. Instead a new church was built in 1821 on the site of the old one on the hill. In 1868 the cornerstone of the present St. Stephen's chuch between Bay and Thorpe was laid by the Dean of York, and on August 3rd, 1870, it was ready for consecration. The brunt of the cost of £6,000 was born by Mr Robert Barry.

The new church, of local stone, is in the geometric Gothic style, giving it the dignfied aspect of a cathedral. Its Norman font was found in a field, where it had been used as a cattle trough, and was brought down from old St. Stephen's.

The older church has a homely interior, with its three decker pulpit and simple pews. It was re-opened in 1943, after several years of disuse. The curious relics hanging from the ceiling, which have intrigued many thousands of visitors, are reminders of an old North Yorkshire custom. They are once-white gloves and garlands, yellowed and blackened by decay, which were carried by two girls at the front of a hearse bearing an unmarried girl's body to church for burial. They were last used here in 1859 at the funeral of Janey Levitt. The garlands generally consisted of two hoops with ribbon and sometimes flower decorations cut from paper. They had a glove suspended in the centre on which was usually written the dead girl's initials and the date. The custom is not peculiar to the district; similar garlands were carried before the coffins of young girls in many other parts of the North. They are possibly a relic of the very old Christian custom of crowning the virgins of the Church with a crown of flowers, as an act of reminder of the Virgin Mary.

The church one might think most in character with the old village is the Congregational Church. One of the largest buildings in the village, its bluff, square frontage is hidden from those passing through the village by the houses in front of it. Its origin can be traced to the influence of a gentleman connected with the Excise Office who came to live in the village and who had previously been a member of the Surrey Chapel, London. It was built in 1840, and the preacher at its opening service was the Reverend John Ely, of Leeds, whose text was 'Thou shalt catch men.'

There is no Roman Catholic church in Fylingdales, but Mass is said regularly at a house close to St. Stephen's. In 1936 the new Methodist Church was opened in Thorpe Lane, also not far from St. Stephen's. It is many years since the Wesleyan Chapel in Chapel Street was used for worship. When it was built, a row of cottages, a road, and finally a grass bank stood between it and the sea. At one time it was also a school. Among those who were taught there was novelist Leo Walmsley. After the last war it was owned for some years by a local architect and his wife, but then, in 1987 the old building re-opened as an exhibition and music centre. The displays explain the local history, geography and ecology of the area and, in the upper part of the building, a newly constructed gallery provides a venue for musical occasions.

The Bay Museum in Fisherhead houses a collection of artefacts and memorabilia built up over the years. The collection is assembled in the old library and reading room built in the 19th century. Prominent in its establishment and progress have been members of the Fylingdales Local History Group, which must be one of the most active of such societies anywhere in the North. Its regular meetings over past years have drawn contributions to original research which have been of inestimable value, and its visiting speakers list is packed with authorities on many subjects.

BAYTOWN TODAY

The short walk along the beach towards Mill Beck is a great tradition for visitors and for residents. Facing south a prospect of the landscape of Peak and moors, patterned with purple and umber, and the great shallow saucers of old alum workings, is attractive in most weathers. The alum was worked here for over 100 years from the middle 17th century and employed about sixty men. The soft brown cliffs as far as Mill Beck constantly run with water for much of the year, and are eroding fast. Further, at Stoupe Brow, there is a firmer and higher cliff, and about this there is a curious story which has gone round the world.

In 1809 a woman and two men travelled in a postchaise from Whitby to Scarborough. The driver climbed from his perch for some reason and the startled horses bolted. All fell over the cliff at Stoupe Brow, not less than 100 feet in height, fifty feet being perpendicular. The chaise turned over three times before crashing to the bottom, but no one was hurt, except that the woman had a scratch or two. They then continued their journey. The story is well authenticated and I have seen it quoted in an American magazine as one of the world's most curious accidents.

As I walked to Mill Beck recently on the return journey along the beach, I saw the old village huddled into its cleft in the steeply rising green hill, and I pondered the changes that had come to Bay. The greatest change took effect slowly after the First World War, when the fishermen left, or died one by one, and the weekenders came. Yet, thanks largely to those cottage owners, the village retains much of its orginal character. To 'freeze' a 17th century village in the physical sense requires a great deal of money, and it is these owners, and the holidaymakers who rent the properties for a summer week or fortnight, who have in nearly every case borne the entire cost. One buyer spent several times the cost of his 17th century home on a solid concrete floor many feet thick, and other renovations. Yet there is no shortage of buyers once a cottage, however tiny, comes on the market. There are in all nearly two hundred cottages at the bottom of the ravine. Most owners are within 100 miles or so, though some live considerably further away. The new influx of cottage owners may have given the village something of a different character, but at least it is a community. If an old 19th century salt found his way down the winding bank again, he would not find too many changes, for the population of Fylingdales has remained pretty constant at about 1,500 since 1801. Most of the solid brick villas of the new village are Victorian, and the rest of the little suburb dates from soon afterwards. With its railway station, inoperative since the line closed in 1965; its big brick hotel, guest houses, its rows of neat semi-detached homes, and its council houses, this is a part of Robin Hood's Bay which is entitled to call itself such by virtue of its postal address, but its links with old Bay are so tenuous as to be almost non-existent.

Only a few yards separate the end of the new village from the beginnings of the old — but it is a separation of many centuries nevertheless. From the top of Bay Bank one looks down on to the crazy triangular pattern formed by box-like stone houses, and red roofs sprouting thin chimney pots. The houses stand on both sides of the ravine. Across to the right, high above them, lies the old red brick coastguard station. Here storm cones were hoisted without the sheltered village below feeling much of the wind. Down the steep twisting road, with its one in three gradient, and over the King's Beck runs New Road, so called after the orginal main street, King Street, mostly fell into the sea in 1780. At the S-bend above the *Laurel Inn,* was the old smith's forge.

The road crosses the stream by a stone bridge, with a farm gate on the right leading up to the coastguard station, also to farmland and a wooded valley. On the right, too, is Bolts House, built in 1709 as an archway over a charming alley known as The Bolts. This is thought to be one route by which men fled to escape the Press Gang and the Excisemen. But there is a Bolts in Scarborough also; the term was used for a narrow trench-like opening between buildings.

Opposite The Bolts almost, climbing along the lip of the ravine like a miniature cornice, is Chapel Street. Near here is Sunny Place, a sheltered nook, and The Openings, which leads to The Square, and Cliff Street. In the garden of Shirley House, the home of an old shipping family, there are figureheads from old whaling ships. Farther up towards the cliff is Tommy Baxter Street, a quaint flower-strewn alley whose name commemorates a great Bay character who died in 1890 or thereabouts. His wife Molly it is said,

King Street

'… the original main street, King Street,
mostly fell into the sea in 1780'.

used to walk to Pickering regularly with a basket of fish. Higher still up the sloping ranks of houses is Silver Street, Martin's Row, and Darnhill Steps, which were not 'downhill' originally, but Daniel's steps. Higher still are rather superior names — Belmont Place, Bloomswell, and The Esplanade. Further along the New Road, nearer to the sea, a narrow path which leads up to the right is known as Jim Bell's Stile (named after a local cabinet maker).

Along this path is Brig Garth, and higher up the hill on this side of the road is a handsome row of cottages known as Fisher Head, in front of which stands the Congregational Chapel. Behind the latter is the village reading room, and a grim little mortuary. Near here there are more 'modern' streets, such as Sunny Side, Littlewood Terrace, and Plane Tree Street. Often the alleys are paved with rocks patterned with interesting fossil shapes. New Road finally winds between rows of large houses of varying periods, many of them now shops. To the right now is Albion Street, leading to cliff and field walks. Once this housed the smallest gas works in Yorkshire, operated by one man. Then, finally, the road runs into The Dock, the open space only a few feet above high water mark. Here the local fox hounds met, and the annual Bay Fair was held every Whitsuntide, with singing and clog dancing contests. The stocks once stood here also.

Which is the oldest house in Baytown, it is impossible to say with accuracy, as so many of them had no deeds, or in some cases the deeds date from many years after the house was built. However, in the mid 1600s, there would already be a respectable number of stone built houses, with thatched roofs.

In The Dock, where once large sailing cobles crowded every foot of room, there is still a space for boats, reserved by the Lord of the Manor in accordance with ancient custom. From here runs King Street, once the most important thoroughfare. In one of these King Street homes is a 100 feet deep well, which is marked on Admiralty charts supposedly. Very little cliff separates the rear of some King Street homes from the sea. It was not always so. King Street was once some distance from the shore, separated from it by a road, another row of cottages and a grass bank. But inch by inch the land fell away, and in 1780 twenty two homes fell on to the shore. Just about the last building to fall was the late Dame Ethel Walker's studio (formerly three 17th century cottages), which was often lashed by spray until it toppled in 1961, only an hour or two after its owners vacated it hurriedly in the middle

The Openings

of the night after hearing a loud crack. Many other cottages perched precariously on the cliff top for decades. In 1974 an ambitious scheme to build a sea wall over 600 feet long on the north side of Wayfoot was completed at a cost in excess of £½ million. This has prevented further erosion of the soft shales and also provided a pleasant and safe walk.

To the south of Wayfoot, a sea wall was built many years ago, an extension of a much older one. Behind the older wall one particularly interesting 17th century house, known now as The Coble, shelters snugly and securely. It was once the home of the chief coastguard officer of Robin Hood's Bay. From what is now a sunny glass-walled lounge, but was formerly a balcony, the old water-guard scanned the horizon through telescopes for sight of smuggling luggers. In more recent years, the coastguards occupied an old building on the north side of this house, one which was pulled down and rebuilt by the University of Leeds in 1965. Here, too, was the old round-house, which served as a bad weather look out post, and a building in which the water-guard, forerunners of the coastguards, kept their boat. When the Duke of Edinburgh, Admiral Commanding Coastguards, arrived at the old station by sea in the early 1880s, a red carpet was laid from the door, down the slipway, to the beach to welcome him.

The university occupied this site as a marine laboratory for over 50 years and pulled down the ancient boathouse to build a laboratory not too dissimilar in appearance, though its many critics complained it was an unlovely box-like structure, destroying the natural balance of the neighbouring cottage. Finally the university closed its research station and the building has since served as a marine activities centre.

There was once a dozen inns in old Baytown. Now there are merely three. These are characterful, to say the least. They are plain, simply and solidly built, modest in some dimensions to the point of crampedness. But they were built for sailors and fishermen, well at home in cramped quarters. The best known pub is the *Bay Hotel* at Wayfoot, where the sea washes its outer wall at high tide. At the bend of New Road, perched near the bridge, is *The Laurel*, with a tiny panelled bar cut out of the sold rock, though the casual visitor would not guess it. At the top of King Street, white walled is *The Dolphin*, which has one of the cosiest parlours in the North. The first mention of any tavern at Robin Hood's Bay was in 1616. At Hutton Bushell Sessions on April 5th of that year, a Bay 'alehouse keeper' was brought before the court for selling ale at 6d per gallon, when the lawful price was 4d.

Also before the court on that day appeared ten other innkeepers of Fylingdales and many from Whitby. I like to think that one of the first inns stood on the site of the old *Bay Hotel,* my favourite English licensed house, certainly possessing one of Yorkshire's finest sea views from its windows. *The Bay* is at least the second inn on this site, a previous one having been washed away by an unusually high tide in 1843. It must be one of the few in England to have had a shipwreck on its very doorstep. During the last century, its window was broken by the bowsprit of a sailing vessel which was swept on to the rocks below.

Another distinction the *Bay Hotel* possesses is that it is one of the places which on occasion has housed the annual meeting of the Court Leet of Fylingdales. This sits annually under its own Seneschal, with its bailiff, foreman, twelve jurymen, two affearors and a moorsman. Most of its business is connected with land enclosures, but it is one of comparatively few Courts Leet in the country, whereas in the 17th century every man in the kingdom lay within the jurisdiction of one.

None of the three inns has any tangible link with the smugglers, but it is certain that their landlords had close connections with them. The pub which figures in the anecdote about the Excisemen who captured illicit cellar stocks, is the *Fishermens Arms* in The Dock, and this dates from 1680. The home for many years of Oliver Storm, the village's last traditional fisherman, and later his widow, its cellar, with its link with other houses, is now filled with concrete. The *Old Mariners,* in The Square, is a house which was an inn until the 1930s, and is a legendary haunt of the smugglers. It is a picturesque old building, with one wall of the old bar parlour covered with Dutch tiles, supposedly brought back as souvenirs by Bay men on smuggling trips. Little John House, near the junction of New Road with The Dock is a former inn, and so also was the old *King's Arms* in King Street, now the Men's Institute. It was to the latter that after the early 19th century battle between a Bay lugger and a customs cutter, an old whaler whose leg had been shot off was brought via an underground passage. The *Old Mariners* was also supposed to have a secret tunnel linking it with the cliff top, as was a house on top of Bay Bank called The Plane Tree, and several cottages. But if all the secret passages that are spoken of really existed, the village would be resting on top of a virtual honeycomb.

It is hardly surprising the old village attracted a colony of artists. Owen Bowen, the famous Yorkshire artist, lived here for some years and was

The Bay Hotel on Lifeboat Day

The Old Coastguard Station

visiting to paint fresh works in his 90s. Perhaps the best known Bay artist was Dame Ethel Walker, a summer resident for many years up to her death in 1950. The regular colony established itself after the First World War, and the Fylingdales Art Group, which still holds annual exhibitions, though usually in Whitby, was founded in 1925. Another well-known artist was Harold Todd, who was the last surviving member of the older colony, and whose pictures still go out all over the world in the form of postcard reproductions. Ulric Walmsley, father of the novelist, lived and painted here. He came from the West Riding of Yorkshire as a young man and gained the unusual distinction of having a picture hung at the Royal Academy when he was 90 years of age. Phil May worked here also, as well as at Whitby.

Now only in the old drawings and paintings can the village be seen in its hey-day when The Dock was full of brown sailed fishing cobles. Occasionally a small pleasure boat sails within the protective arm of Ness Point; and coasters, oil barges and steamers of many sizes traverse the waters between the headlands in mechanical succession. Once in a while, a brightly painted keel boat from a not too distant port creeps into the bay, casts down its pots, and is off within minutes, leaving slender black markers bobbing on the waves. But the village will always look lonely, like deserted fishing villages all over Britain, without its cobles. Not only fishing boats and smuggling luggers berthed. Trading vessels of all kinds called, and at Wayfoot in the late 18th century there was a wooden wharf known as Bulmer's Staith.

A regular visitor to the bay was the coal ketch from Hartlepool, which beached on The Landing for only one tide. It took skilled seamanship, and as soon as it grounded, carts began unloading the coal. Often a whole winter's stock had to be bought at once. A packet used to sail from Scarborough to Hartlepool and pick up passengers off the bay. Below Peak Cliffs, a channel was cut into the rock to allow small ships to load alum. Lime for the farmers, as well as grain for the mill, came here by sea.

Long after the old sailing and fishing days, a number of retired mariners helped Bay to retain its character. Some of them called their homes after the ships they mastered. In one Bay alley is a cottage named *Coralline* after a brig of Hartlepool, built in 1857. In Thorpe is a house named *Marmion,* and a brig of that name foundered in the Gulf of Riga in 1858. Often the cottages could be lonely homes for women — for a Bay wife might not see her husband for long periods, perhaps for several years, when he went to sea. One old captain, who gave up his command at seventy one, after the Second World

Reuben Storm

'An old sailor who claimed to have made
the last voyage in the last sailing ship
registered in these parts'.

War, was able to retire to a house he bought when he married at twenty six, but in which he had not spent more than a few consecutive weeks in all the intervening years.

An old sailor who claimed to have made the last voyage in the last sailing ship registered in these parts was Reuben Storm. In 1910, he sailed in the vessel from the Tees to London, with a cargo, and then returned to Hartlepools in ballast. In 1933, when he was past his eightieth birthday, he recalled nostalgically:

> *'How the old place has changed. Visitors from the towns — why, we hardly ever saw any. The village used to be filled with young sailors on leave in winter. They had some lively times.'*

The old characters who can bring back the old days have nearly all gone. The charm of the village is as subtle and insidious as ever.

LEO WALMSLEY

an one genuinely rationalise affection for such a community when one is not of it, and never can be, because so much of it truly belongs to the past? The answer must be that fortunately one can come extremely close to it because of the writings of the late Leo Walmsley, the author who came to live there as a small child, and whose biographical novels reflect the life and times of the old fishing community whose last years he shared.

This book has been concerned with that community, rather than individuals. But as Leo in life wrote the foreword to it, perhaps these final pages may be allowed to express briefly words of thanks for his unique and lasting contribution towards understanding those who lived and worked here, and appreciating this beautiful and fascinating section of Yorkshire coast, with its hinterland of valleys and moorland.

Leo Walmsley was born in 1892 in Shipley, West Yorkshire, and brought to the village by his parents at the age of two. He died in Cornwall in 1966. Absent from 'T'awd spot' (as he learned from its natives to term it), exiled he never was, for in his heart he lived there every day.

His books immortalised the inshore fishermen of Bay, and reflected their character with unerring accuracy. Born Lionel Walmsley (his father Ulric was both artist and photographer), he was educated at a village school, and at Scarborough, becoming a pupil teacher in North Yorkshire, an occupation he did not like and later confessed he would have abandoned and gone to sea, but for his mother.

The humble home where he and his family lived in King Street carries a plaque above the door. He left that home to serve with distinction in World War One. In East Africa he won the Military Cross for bravery as an observer over enemy lines. After the war he left the village to live and work in London as a freelance writer of adventure and natural history books and articles. There he married for the first time, and when some years later the marriage

Leo Walmsley with two wounded Belgian soldiers 24th October, 1914

ended, returned to Bay to live as a fisherman, writing little or nothing. It was not until 1932 when he was 40 years old, that he produced *Three Fevers*, the novel which later became the film *Turn of the Tide*, the first film Arthur Rank made. In the following seven years, the books which set the seal on his reputation as a novelist — *Phantom Lobster*, *Foreigners*, *Sally Lunn*, and *Love in the Sun* — followed. In 1944 came his autobiography *So Many Loves*, still one of the most charmingly written of all his works in many peoples' opinion.

After some years in Fowey, he returned to live in a house on the moor behind the village but left at the outbreak of World War Two to live in Wales, with his second wife Margaret. When this marriage also ended, he moved to Fowey again to live in a hut on a creek in which he had written *Three Fevers*. Here he was to produce more novels, and find happiness with Stephanie, his third wife, who bore him his last child Selina.

Yet like that Yorkshire beach he loved, and which remains largely unchanged, so did his own youthful and vigorous spirit remain almost to his death, surprising many who met him for the first time. On his last visit to that beach, while on a working holiday, one October morning on a walk beyond Mill Beck, finding himself alone, he took off his clothes and swam in the cold North Sea. That walk on a dazzlingly sunny morning was, he told me later, the 'most extraordinary experience' of his life.

He did not offer further explanation but I guessed then, and wrote a few months later, hearing of his death, that he had met again that same barefoot boy who had revelled in the seashore, and become captivated by it nearly seventy summers before.

Leo's original ambition was to become a marine biologist. Instead his pen was to kindle the curiosity and affection of many thousands for his beloved village.

A year or two before the first edition of this book was completed and published we met for the first time when I went to interview him for the *Yorkshire Evening Post*. We became friends and both corresponded and met in Cornwall and in Yorkshire over the years that were left to him. I was impressed to find his passion for the very stones of those houses by the shore blazed as passionately as though he had left it the previous month, instead of having been half way round the world and living in far off places for most of the past half century.

To encourage and maintain interest in the works of Leo and his artist father Ulric, the Walmsley Society was founded in the early 1980s. With members not only in Yorkshire, but all over the country, and indeed in several countries, including America, Canada, and New Zealand, it meets usually in the spring at Robin Hood's Bay, and in the south of England in the autumn, but on occasion in London and other areas associated with the author.

Thus many years after Leo Walmsley portrayed the lives of the inshore fishermen, his writings still play an important role in reminding a vast multitude of the beauties of this unique curve in the Yorkshire coast, majestic in storm, and in sunshine colourful and kindly to even the smallest visitor. And while bygone days can be fascinating, Bay offers so much to the present, not only educating fresh generations to the mysteries and excitements of the seashore, but banishing city cares for their elders with cliff and meadow walks. Of all our jewels in North Yorkshire, many would say this is the fairest and brightest of all.

CHANGING TIMES

ince this book was first revised in 1990, two major changes have taken place in Bay, both of which have had a significant impact on the village. The incessant pounding of the North Sea at the base of the cliffs and the rainwater draining from the fields above have continued the process of erosion which has been going on for millennia. Earlier sea defences, the last completed in 1974, have been effective in protecting the village but erosion has eaten into the unprotected cliffs on either side threatening to encircle the houses close to the shore. A new sea defence scheme completed in 2001 at a cost in excess of £3 million has given Bay another lease of life for an estimated 50 years.

When the sea wall was built in the early 1970s it was amongst the first in the country to employ a new concept in design. Rather than having a flat front facing the sea the wall was contoured along the face of the existing cliff thus reducing wave refraction.

By the late 1990s design had once again moved on. The new technique was to place huge boulders along the base of the cliffs and allow the gaps between to absorb some of the impact of the waves. Hundreds of boulders each weighing many tonnes were ferried by barge across the North Sea from Norway, dropped on the beach and then individually placed in position along the base of the cliffs. In addition to this 'rock armour', extensive drainage, grading and piling work was undertaken to reduce the likelihood of slumping of clay on the upper cliffs.

The visual impact on the village of this work has been pronounced, and not to everybody's liking. None the less, a new access to the village and the northern shore has been created which will benefit boat owners and those visitors who were previously often cut off by a rising tide!

The second change to impact on the village has been the conversion of the old coastguard station in The Dock into an interpretative and visitor centre. The present building is at least the third to occupy this site over the past few hundred years. Records show that in the early 1800s the building then on the site was in use as a public house that was later converted into three tenements. In March 1829 the recently established coastguard service took over the use of the building and they continued in occupation until they moved, in the early 1900s, into the purpose built station on Fisher Head.

The building once again reverted to accommodation and in 1910 is recorded in a Finance Act survey as being used for holiday lets. It is possible that at about this time the building was hired by Walter Garstang, first Professor of Zoology at Leeds University, in order to accommodate some of his students who were studying marine biology. In May 1912 Professor Garstang together with Professor Denny of Sheffield University persuaded the two universities to hire the building for use as a marine laboratory. The annual rent was to be £8 and upkeep not to exceed £10! The building would be known by the rather grand title of the Yorkshire Universities Marine Laboratory.

Accommodation consisted of a laboratory in the old watchhouse and a cottage next door. The laboratory was a long narrow room with low ceiling, two windows (plus one with a small shuttered hole for the coastguard's telescope) and was slightly curved in line with the sea wall below; it had a wide bench "*like the bar of a railway refreshment room*" running the whole length of the front wall and with a sink at one end.

In 1916 the university was offered the opportunity to purchase the property but was "disinclined" to buy, and a seven year lease was agreed at £18 per year. At some time during the First World War, a machine gun was placed on the wall outside the building; a request was sent to the War Office in March 1919, asking that the machine gun emplacement be removed because "*it interferes with useful space*".

In May 1922 Professor Garstang pleaded with the university to take up its option to purchase the property and the following July this was agreed "*after Professor Kendall had given his opinion that it was unlikely to fall into the sea*". The purchase price was £220 and a further £60 was agreed for improvements to be carried out. The university surveyor saw this as "A *good investment if nothing else*".

The arrangement with Sheffield University was ended in 1928 and Professor Garstang retired in 1933. With the increasing demands on space there was an opportunity to purchase the adjacent building. Professor Gilligan of the Geology Department was asked to comment on the possible purchase. He reported that the cliffs were eroding so rapidly that the cottage was threatened with destruction in the very near future, and concluded that *"neither this property nor even the Marine Station itself can be regarded as definitely safe, and it is a risk for students to be housed there"*. The university sent this report to various authorities, urging prompt action – *"It would appear that the whole of the land and house property is in serious danger . . . (and) . . . is likely to slip into the sea in the near future"*. The 'authorities' appear to have taken little notice as the Quarterdeck was not constructed until the mid 1960s.

During the war the building was taken over by the War Department and afterwards use of the laboratory remained at a *"low ebb"*. 1960 saw the arrival of Professor Dodd who, together with Dr Lewis, began exploring the possibility of rebuilding the laboratory as a permanent marine station with resident staff. A grant from the Wellcome Trust enabled work to commence in 1964 but this was not completed until 1966 and was formally opened in April 1967. One of the innovations of the new laboratory was the installation in the basement of an 8,000 gallon sea water tank fed by water pumped in from an inlet some 150 yards down the shore. From this tank sea water could be circulated to the various aquaria throughout the building. In 1968 the building was entered for a Civic Trust Award and received a commendation for *"the contribution it makes to the appearance of the local scene . . . there is a seamanlike robustness of character which adds interest to this coastal village scene and seems to belong to it happily"*. Not everybody agreed with this accolade.

From the mid 1960s until its closure in 1982 the laboratory was principally used as a research establishment with 90 scientific papers being published during that time. A full economic enquiry into the viability of the laboratory was carried out in the late 1970s and in spite of a report to the university senate which showed it to be an efficient, productive and low cost department, the university decided to close the laboratory as an economic measure. This was *"short sighted and ill advised"* according to some of those involved.

The building was eventually sold and for some years used as a private management training business. On the market again in the late 1990s the property was purchased by the National Trust for conversion to a visitor and education centre. With the benefit of a local legacy, the Trust was able to consider completely demolishing the existing building and rebuilding to an external design reminiscent of the earlier coastguard station. After much careful research, plans were approved that would see the new building echoing that of the early 20th century.

Opened in conjunction with the North York Moors National Park Authority on Friday, 13th October 2000, the building houses a self catering flat on the top floor with an education and meeting room below. The ground floor is devoted to an interpretative centre in which the elements of the surrounding coastline and sea are explored through a series of models, panels, and hands-on displays.

In 1913 Leo Walmsley was paid 5/– (25p) a week to look after the marine laboratory and help collect specimens from the beach. In his book "*So Many Loves*" Walmsley describes his work at the lab: "*It wasn't the actual spotting and identification of the specimens that was so exciting. It was the seeing of them up close for the first time*". I think he would have approved the present design and use of the new building.

Alan Staniforth
November 2003